Special Limited Edition

Thank you for
purchasing my book

Every penny goes
towards to the Hospice

This is book number

177 of 400

_____
Trudy

With just 25p

St Lukes Hospice
A story of faith

in God and people

by

Trudy Westmore-Cox

With just 25p
St Lukes Hospice
A story of faith
in God and people

by Trudy Westmore-Cox

Inquiries should be addressed to
PB Software
3 Nelson Road
Ashingdon, Rochford
Essex SS4 3EJ

FIRST EDITION
First Printing June 2010
by
4edge Ltd
7a Eldon Way
Eldon Way Industrial Estate
HOCKLEY, Essex SS5 4AD.
Tel 01702 200243

A CIP catalogue record of this book
is available from the British Library

ISBN 978-0-9565891-0-1

Cover designed by: PB Software

Dedication

This book is dedicated first and foremost to my late husband, Les Cox. Without his constant support, encouragement and help St. Luke's would not have happened.

It is also dedicated to my children, grandchildren, family and friends, who never stopped supporting me throughout the years to make this special House on the Hill - St. Luke's Hospice - possible. I will never forget their patience and tolerance with me.

It is dedicated to all our fundraisers and supporters who have kept faith in the vision of the hospice.

It is dedicated to those of our early fundraisers who have sadly died but did so much to make St. Luke's become a reality.

It is also dedicated to all my patients and their families whom I have felt privileged to care for.

None of it would have been possible without the generosity of Harry Bacon, Mark Gallagher and Malcolm Mathers and the Board Members of Basildon Corporation. They listened to my 'plea for help' and 'my story' to establish a home for cancer patients and their families.

A Message from Trudy

Trudy Westmore-Cox

For many years I have been encouraged to write a book about St. Luke's but have always shied away from it.

There are so many emotions connected with the hospice story. The reason why it had to happen; the planning and development; the needs of so many people. To do the story justice much of the credit must go to our wonderful community. So many people came along, listened to my 'story' and then joined the now famous hospice family.

Writing the hospice story burdened me but, at the same time, the journey of St. Luke's was such a privilege and a most humbling experience I have ever had.

I love telling the story. As I remember the events I experience the story coming to life all over again but writing it down is a different matter. Will it come to life for you reading it? Because of the enormity of the task I am nervous.

With God's help, and the help and support of the people who were with me right at the beginning, I will try my very best to tell this wonderful miracle story.

To everyone who helped and supported us - a great big 'thank you' and God bless. But, most of all, I thank God for the vision of St. Luke's, for health, strength, staying power and for Him answering so many prayers and for making the 25p grow into the miracle of St. Luke's.

Co-founder & Patron St. Luke's

The Bishop of Bradwell, Dr. Laurie Green

Dr. Laurie Green

This is a story of courage against all the odds. In these pages you will read the story and see the illuminating pictures of a piece of Essex history which defies all expectation.

The story of St. Luke's Hospice proves that even when all seems against us, with vision, determination and the support of friends and the Almighty, everything is possible. Those of us who have had the honour and joy of knowing Trudy and helping, even in the smallest way, in the development and the work of St. Luke's Hospice, will testify to her amazing resolve and fortitude in the face of untold difficulties which brought into being a hospice which itself is a centre of excellence - the sort of excellence which can proceed only from a deep love for those who reach out to us for help in their time of need.

Trudy it was who saw the need and was so determined to respond to it that, despite many a setback and the refusal of some to support her, she won through so that now Basildon has a hospice which has brought many new friends together, has been a tower of strength to families in their moments of deepest need and despair, and remains as a sign of peace, love and hope at the heart of our community.

Thank you Trudy, and all those in your wonderful team, for giving us St. Luke Hospice.

Bishop of Bradwell.

The Book

This story is written in great detail because every milestone, every event, was a great achievement, involving many people - most of whom gave their time voluntarily.

Each event tells its own story: happy stories, sad stories, emotional stories.

So many times the prayer chain worked overtime but even at difficult times we knew God was with us and that assurance was a great comfort.

The stories are presented as separate chapters. In this way the reader may only want to read the parts that interest them rather than every word.

It is the story of a great community: Thurrock, Basildon, Wickford and Billericay.

I feel very proud and privileged to be part of this great community.

The photographs of patients, children, parents and others involved with the hospice have all been taken with their permission or with the understanding that they may be used for teaching purposes and for the Hospice Story Book.

My thanks to everyone of you who allowed me to share the hospice story in picture and text.

Acknowledgements

To my husband Derek, without whose typestting skills and typing all the pages ready for publication this book would not have happened.

To Keith and Richard for proof reading and meticulously correcting the pages.

To Paul for his technical expertise and patience inhelping us to get it ready for printing.

Who Am I ?

I arrived in England in 1955 as an 18 year old from Germany I came straight from school to start my training as a general nurse at the Metropolitan Hospital in the East End of London.

My sister, Irmgard, had made the same decision six months prior. I joined her at 'The Met' (as it was affectionately known by the local people).

I felt terribly homesick but she was a great comforter. The first ward I worked on was the children's ward. I was so glad because I just love children.

Me and my sister Irmgard

Children's ward at the 'Met'

Shortly after qualifying as a staff nurse I met my future husband, Les, who was a patient at the Metropolitan Hospital. We married and we had two little boys, Michael and Keith.

Both babies were born in the Mothers Salvation Army Hospital in Hackney, London.

When Keith was 5 weeks old, in 1961, we were able to move as so many Eastenders before us, to the then 'New Town' of Basildon.

Every year after this move I attended the annual reunion at the hospital where I met fellow nurses who trained with me.

Each time after these reunions I came home sad, missing my colleagues and patients terribly. They say: 'Once a nurse, always a nurse' and there is some truth in that.

Someone suggested to me to try night duty at our then local hospital in Billericay, St. Andrews. But I didn't want to leave the children in someone else's care.

I eventually went to see the Matron at St. Andrews who offered me two nights at the weekend so that while I was working, Les, my husband, could care for the boys.

During that time on night duty I met Jackie, who was about to leave the hospital and to start her training as a District Nurse, or Queen's Nurse as they were known.

At that time I had no idea what District Nurses did.

She explained it to me and said that when you were trained it would fit in well with caring for the children once they are at school.

I continued working as a night staff nurse at St. Andrews until my brother, Gerold, asked me if I would help him.

He wanted to go to Nepal and work there, supported by a world organisation called 'Bread for the World'.

We decided he and Ingrid, his wife, would live with us. He managed to get work with the removal firm Jeakins from Laindon and Ingrid looked after Michael and Keith while I did my training as a District Nurse in Barking and Leytonstone.

Following training I applied for a post in Basildon and they accepted me, providing I passed my driving test as Basildon was classed as a 'rural area'.

By now the children had started school and we were able to manage the children's needs around my working hours. It worked fine except Keith kept running home from school and I often started my working day with hidden tears, worrying about my little boy.

I was able also to collect them from school and stay at home with them until Les arrived home from Billericay (where he worked as a manager at Billericay Service Station). He then took over and I continued with my work which often meant going out on night cases.

Thus my District Nursing career began and altogether I worked for the Health Authority as a sister in the community for 26 years.

During my time as a District Nurse we were blessed with another little baby boy in January 1972.

Now we had three lovely boys - Michael, Keith and Christopher.

Working on the District

As a very busy District Nurse with 26 years experience (1963-1989) I was often saddened by the fact that the pressure and volume of work (an average of 20 patients per day) did not allow for any extra time to be spent with our patients, to talk, to listen, and to comfort them.

They were given the best possible care we were able to offer but, often, they were on their own, sad and distressed and needing more than just nursing care.

Patients and their families had many questions and wanted to talk about their feelings, worries and anxieties. This in turn required extra time from the nurse which was just not available.

Sister Trudy Cox

I met with many dedicated carers, family and friends who so desperately needed a break and someone to support them during the difficult and stressful times. There was no-one who could take over the care of their loved ones and so they struggled on, scared, exhausted, feeling very much alone, unaware of the help available to them.

Worse still was seeing a patient crying out in unbearable pain which no-one seemed to be able to ease or control. This brought extra worry and distress to those caring for the patient.

As a nurse I find it very difficult to see anyone suffer, always have done. I became a nurse knowing that this vocation would give me the opportunity to do my bit to help and support patients during difficult times.

Often after such visits I would drive my car where no-one could see me and cry my eyes out because of the helplessness of wishing I could have helped them more, easing their pain and suffering. then tried to pull myself together and wash my face which, of course, was red and my eyes swollen, and, with the help of a little make-up, started off again to visit the next patient.

My feelings of sadness and frustration as well as helplessness had to be buried for the moment, but they never went totally away. I just couldn't understand why more couldn't be done.

In those days (the 60's and 70's and early 80's) we District Nurses had no special training to deal with severe and difficult to control pains nor communication skills. All we could do was to try and support and help each other. I was fortunate to work with a very caring team of nursing colleagues. When one of us felt down, the others were there with help, support and advice.

People often say, 'I suppose you get used to it and maybe get hardened to it'. Well, even at my ripe old age of 70 years plus I am still as sensitive as ever so I don't think I will change any more now.

My heart also went out to the bereaved - those trying to adjust to their new situation and trying to come to terms with the death of a loved one. How sad it is when families and friends are grieving for the one they love. They too need someone to listen, someone to share their grief with, to be sad with them, and to understand and support them with all their different emotional feelings.

For many years I pondered, inwardly knowing I was called to do something more for these dear people who suffered so much. In those days I didn't know much about hospice care. I knew about St. Joseph's in Hackney and, like most people, I thought hospices cared only for patients in the last few days or weeks of their life and that patients were admitted to a hospice to die. Whenever one of my patients went to St. Joseph's they certainly never came back home.

I kept hoping that someone would do something to help us care for patients with cancer and help and support their families. But nothing ever changed and we nurses just soldiered on again and again, as no-one else came forward, I felt drawn to do something to ease these situations.

I heard about the Royal Marsden Hospital in London that specialised for cancer patients. I applied to the Education Department there to attend a course in Palliative Care. I was fortunate enough to be accepted.

Then, one Christmas Eve, I knew exactly what I had to do

To put you in the picture, I should explain that Christmas Eve is a very special time for us in Germany (my home country). When I married, my husband and I brought that custom into our newly married life so that as my three sons grew up they were always very excited on the day leading up to Christmas.

On Christmas Eve the sitting room was out of bounds to the children, and their excitement grew as Les and I prepared the Christmas room together for them.

Finally we would ring the little bell and the children were allowed to enter the Christmas room where candles were flickering everywhere, the Christmas tree and crib ready to be admired, and Christmas songs playing in the background.

On one particular Christmas Eve we were almost ready to ring the Christmas bell when the telephone rang and I was called out to go to see a patient suffering from cancer.

The children were disappointed, but I reassured them that I would not be gone long.

When I reached the patient's house and entered the bedroom, I saw the patient in bed, apparently asleep, with her two little girls who were just 5 and 7 years old, sitting on the floor by the bed watching television.

I walked forward and realised the patient was not sleeping but had died, and it was at that moment that the door opened and her 15 year old son came in carrying a Christmas Tree.

I telephoned the father of the 15 year old boy to collect him and then took the two little girls to my home for my husband to care for them.

I returned to see my patient feeling very sad knowing that she died so alone without being supported by us, the caring profession. (This was the first time I had 'met' her and it was too late).

She may not have had any physical pain but she must have worried about who will look after her children them, care for them and love them.

As I drove home I again battled with all my emotions and frustrations.

Why weren't we nurses called earlier? Where were the other professionals?

I just couldn't understand why we were not called to care for her, to give her the care she needed and support her during her final days.

Coming back home we celebrated Christmas the best we could. When all the children were finally asleep, I knew once again that something had to be done. This was not right.

I finally made up my mind to open a home for cancer patients and their families. I should not wait any longer.

My husband, Les, promised to support and help. He, like me, felt that it was appalling that so little was done for dying patients.

In the New Year I was called to another patient and on entering the house I found a man in his late fifties or early sixties, crying out in pain calling, "Sister, put me down. You wouldn't let an animal suffer like this".

These heartbreaking experiences only served to strengthen me in my resolve to do more for these patients. So St. Luke's was 'born' on Christmas Eve many years ago.

Where to go from here ?

Following that Christmas Eve filled with many emotions I really now wanted to put into practice what I felt I had been called to do many months ago.

I still hoped that someone would come forward to help establish a home for cancer patients and their families where patients and their families would find love and help with understanding and skilled people who knew how to help with pain and symptom control sometimes, or rather more often, unbearable pain.

Time could be spent with them rather than the rushed care which so often happens in busy hospitals where symptoms could be addressed and controlled before they became so unbearable. Where patients would be treated with dignity and individual care, to live out the remainder of their lives still enjoying being around and not wasting away waiting to die.

But how? Who would help? Whom should I approach? Where do I start ? Where better to start than with family and friends.

My husband, Les, had known for years how upset I was about the suffering of my patients, how disillusioned I was about some of the treatment and the lack of help and professional support.

Following that momentous Christmas Eve we talked and talked again or, rather, I talked and he listened.

I had such a strong call to do something. To me it seemed so simple at the time. (Little did I know how wrong I was). Les was willing to support me, to be part of establishing a home for cancer patients and their families.

We both agreed if it was the money that stopped us we would give up our house to raise the necessary funds. We both realised that it wouldn't be easy.

It would be hard work and a very big commitment. We were both also anxious that the children were our first responsibility and that they should not suffer.

Finance wasn't the big problem. We never had much anyway but gave them a happy home.

They were contented children, and from early on they were aware of how fortunate they were being healthy and surrounded by loving parents.

Our camping holidays were always the highlight in the summer holidays, either in Wales or the Lake District, climbing or swimming, or at the seaside.

The children would have to be consulted and had to be happy about sharing the vision of a home for cancer patients.

As a District Nurse on call 24 hours, they were used to me having to go out at a moment's notice. Les's work as manager of a garage was more regular, and also with the help and support of an au-pair girl during summer and Easter holidays we all felt life wouldn't change that much.

The children were happy and eager to help. Hmm, how naïve we all were, especially me. Les agreed to take on most of the home responsibilities and background work. He did not want to be involved in giving talks or public engagements, which we knew we had to do in order to get help and support.

He was a very private man, but very office orientated, which was a great help, as I am not much of an office person, more a 'people's person'.

How glad and relieved I was that he was so correct in all to do with office work — hence he became the administrator.

He helped me out many a time when I lost an important piece of paper. He always copied and filed everything. I will be forever grateful to him for keeping me in order which, I readily agree, could not have been easy for him.

That Christmas Eve the vision of a home for cancer patients and their families finally started to become a reality.

So, you the reader, please remember that Christmas Eve is very, very special. It is the beginning of a dream and vision - 'St. Luke's Hospice'.

Minnie and the first 25p

Minnie was one of my patients whom I visited as a District Nurse. Because she was paralysed, she was either bed or chair bound and often in great pain and discomfort. She felt isolated and distressed, and totally consumed by her situation.

Minnie lived with her husband who cared for her in between District Nurse and Home Help visits.

Occasionally, family and friends would call but these visits were often difficult and short as Minnie found it so hard to be cheerful and welcoming.

As nurses, we tried hard to interest her in the outside world - giving her something else to think about.

The only things she really did like was playing Scrabble with her husband and knitting but this was often interrupted by pain and discomfort.

One day I shared with Minnie the vision of a Home for Cancer Patients and their families.

Without naming any of the patients she could tell how much I was affected by the sadness of it all. Minnie showed great interest and wanted to help.

I told her about the Christmas Eve - the children who had to be taken into care as their mother had died. How lonely and worried she must have been about what would happen to her children and who would care for them.

Minnie listened intently and then with tears in her eyes gave me the now very famous 25p as a token to start a Home For Cancer patients and their families.

I then asked her if she wanted to help me. How, was her instant reply?

I thought about it for a moment and told her I needed to write many letters to share the vision with others and this was taking up a lot of my time.

Would she like to become my volunteer 'secretary'. If she could address and stamp the envelopes all I needed to do was to post them.

She was getting very excited about helping me so together we teamed up. She worked for hours and this in turn helped her to forget (for a little while) her own situation.

I then gently pushed her a little further. Minnie was a great knitter and often showed me little tricks of the trade. How would you feel, I asked her, if I invited a few friends to her home and together we could knit and sew and then try to sell the items.

Minnie asked me straight away to get some wool for her and, as we were approaching Easter, she started knitting Easter decorations, little chicks in their baskets.

She did even more than that. Whenever somebody visited she made them buy her goods: doctors, nurses, home helps and any visitors were soon bullied by her to buy not only for themselves but also for their friends and families.

I had no idea what a 'business women' she really was, and it didn't take long before a group of us were sitting in her sitting room working hard at our 'handicrafts' with Minnie as our teacher.

Minnie

So the first 'fundraising house group' started in Minnie's sitting room. Her poor husband put up with us all but you could tell how glad he was to see Minnie so involved and much happier.

Minnie, by helping others, helped herself, and often told us how much more she got out of it than she put in.

> **"From now on it was a case of real team work."**

* Bill Freeman, manager of Essex Papers, allowed me to look around his paper factory and take as much A4 paper as I needed for my letters.

* Colin Wind, a local pharmist and dear friend, made his photocopier in his shop available to copy my letters.

* Grace, from Social Services, helped by making more copies on her office photocopier.

Colin and Bill

* Minnie, as my volunteer secretary, put the letters in envelopes, sealed them and put the stamps on. It was with much pride I then took the letters to the post office for posting.

Our little circle of hospice workers was complete. It was wonderful to meet these people and for them to offer their help without any thought of payment for the time they spent helping me.

First meeting at Clay Hill Road

In April 1983, together with Les and the children we organised a meeting at home, inviting friends, members of our family, colleagues, doctors, nurses, social workers, and health visitors, people I had worked with and got to know as a District Nurse.

We were approximately 40 people in our sitting room in Clay Hill Road, Basildon, with Minnie's 25p lying for all to see in the middle.

I shared with them some of my experiences as a District Nurse, and how I felt that God had called me to help patients suffering from cancer and their families. God had given a vision of a Home for Cancer Patients and their families.

I told them about my feelings of sadness and frustration, of being alone at times and angry, and how awful it was to see patients die alone in pain, and families not knowing what to do. Families letting out their concern and frustration at us as District Nurses, and they are nervous to share their feelings with their doctors.

That day on the floor in our sitting room with Minnie's 25p in the middle, we all were unanimous that something should, could and would be done.

All those present were happy and willing to support us as a family but felt we should not give up our house.

That evening we decided that we should have a small management committee to discuss things further, and to share with the community at large, and our thoughts and plans of a Home for Cancer Patients and their families.

As far as the children were concerned, we had to be open with them. Our first priority now had to be with our children. They already knew how unhappy I was at times, suffering with my patients, so they wanted to help but both Michael and Keith were concerned for us.

First visit to St. Joseph's Hospice

Would it be too much? How would it affect our home life? How about little Christopher? If we lived with sick and dying patients would we have to be always quiet? Would our happy home become a sad one?

I told them of visits I had made to St. Joseph's Hospice and that the Mother Superior had invited us as a family for 'tea', so that the children would and could feel comfortable once they could see for themselves that hospices (as houses for cancer patients were known) weren't necessarily sad places. So off we went on a visit to St. Joseph's.

The Mother Superior had prepared a welcoming tea and in no time at all the children felt at ease. Michael and Keith had many questions while Christopher played happily with his football in the corridor while the patients watched him.

From little children all three boys were used to seeing patients. They often accompanied me as a District Nurse (in those days things were much more relaxed).

The children would be hugged and spoiled by the patients and their families, playing in the gardens and enjoying cakes and fruit, while I looked after the patient.

The visit to St. Joseph's eased their concerns so we went home knowing the children felt comfortable and wanted to help.

Keith's Album

As a birthday present in September 1984, my son, Keith gave me a very special gift.

He presented me with an album containing records of the first year of the 'Hospice Story'.

I've selected a few of the first album pages here. Some encouraging and some not.

'Gott Kann', a faded card with the words. 'God Can' in German is the centre of the first page. "Yes, God can and God did".

Keith, unbeknown to me, had borrowed my diary where I had made my first entries, starting in 1983.

This was the year I first made it public that, together with Les, my late husband, we wanted to open a home where we could care for cancer patients and their families.

"The beginning of the venture....

"A District Nursing Sister, Trudy Cox, had for a few years pondered the idea of opening a hospice for the terminally ill in Basildon .

"It was in the early months of 1983 that she made public her wish to open a hospice.

"A lot of people thought it was a very good idea....."

"With only a vision to drive her on the support of family and friends was worth its weight in gold.

"The Helen Steiner Rice poem was sent to her by her colleagues and typified the belief in her that others had.

"Early encouragement came from all over Basildon ....."

"Climb 'till your dream comes true"
Often your tasks will be many,
And more than you think you can do -
Often the road will be rugged
And the hills insurmountable, too -
But always remember, the hills ahead
Are never as steep as they seem,
And with Faith in your heart start upward
And climb 'till you reach your dream,
For nothing in life that is worthy
Is ever too hard to achieve
If you have the courage to try it
And you have the Faith to believe -
For Faith is a force that is greater
Than knowledge or power or skill
And many defeats turn to triumph
If you trust in God's wisdom and will -
For Faith is a mover of mountains,
There's nothing that God cannot do,
So start out today with Faith in your heart
And "Climb Till Your Dream Comes True"!

Another of Keith's album pages contained the newspaper cutting shown here. Keith words were:-

'The bitter-sweet pill of media coverage. The very first newspaper story about the hospice.'

'On Monday, April 25th 1983, this article appeared in the 'Evening Echo.'

'Although the publicity was welcome the sensationalism was not. Sister Cox's diary for this day reads 'felt very low.'

Les and I had not wanted that to become public knowledge. We wanted it to be a silent gift to the hospice. It made us sad that our wishes were not respected.

Keith also records another hurtful time when we were accused of using hospice funds for personal gain.

I'll sell up to help dying says Trudy

A NURSE is prepared to sell her Basildon home to help the town get a hospice.

Community sister, Mrs Trudy Cox, 47, of Clay Hill Road, says she has had a calling to try to get a place where people can die with dignity and free from pain.

She said: "I've always been interested in terminally ill patients. At the moment, some have a little bit of a rough deal as the nearest hospice is St Joseph's in Hackney.

"Most people would hope to die at home in the bosom of their family, but that is not always possible.

"A hospice provides a special sort of nursing care where drugs are given little and often to control pain."

Mrs Cox, who has three sons, aged 24, 22 and 11, finally decided to do something constructive when two of her patients had to be sent to the Hackney hospice because there was nowhere nearer.

She said: "Basildon Hospital is very good, but they're too busy to concentrate on any one patient."

Mrs Cox contacted a Billericay estate agency to see if it had any properties suitable for conversion.

The agent contacted Basildon Development Corporation, and now Mrs Cox is hoping the corporation will help find somewhere.

She has contacted doctors, district nurses and organisers of other hospices and 40 people turned up when she held meeting in her house last week.

Mrs Cox said: "The response so far has been great. I feel as if I've had a calling. There's no doubt that there is a need in Basildon.

"I'm so involved. My husband and are prepared to sell our home to raise money. All I have is my house and goodwill."

Mrs Cox said that if a suitable property, with planning permission could be found soon, the hospice could open in 18 months.

She said: "My idea would be to start with about four beds and expand as the need arises. I think it is best to get going rather than spend a lot of time fund raising.

"Otherwise, we'll be the first patients."

Another meeting has been arranged for June 6 at Vange Health Centre where doctors, councillors and other interested people will be invited, and a committee elected.

Then Mrs Cox hopes to call a public meeting in Basildon.

A Basildon Development Corporation spokesman said: "We're prepared to help her as far as we can."

7

Note from Dr. David Frampton

Following these newspaper reports and accusations I returned home tired and discouraged, to find a magazine and a note on my doorstep.

The note was from Dr. David Frampton, the Medical Director, whom I had first met at St. Joseph's.

It encouraged me and renewed my belief in the project simply because someone else shared my vision.

God's timing again was perfect.

Both Les and I asked God again and again for His guidance, for health and strength and wisdom.

Thank you, David.

Dr David Frampton was closely associated with Basildon Hospice, advising it when it first got off the ground because he was then a consultant at St. Joseph's, the famous East End hospice where the movement began.

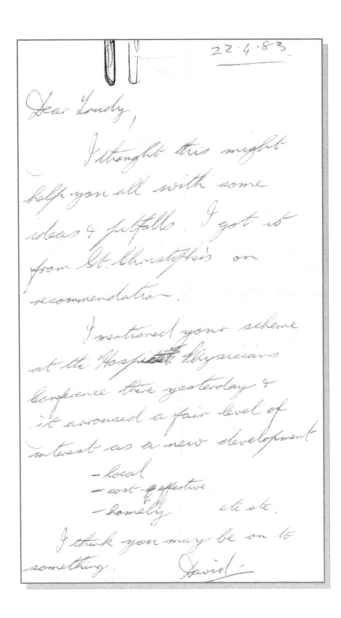

22.4.83

Dear Lindy,

I thought this might help you all with some ideas & pitfalls. I got it from St. Christopher's on recommendation.

I mentioned your scheme at the Hospital Physicians' Conference there yesterday & it aroused a fair level of interest as a new development
– local
– cost-effective
– homely etc etc.

I think you may be on to something.

David

The words of the following hymn always confirmed and encouraged me. I didn't know how it would all happen but what I did know was that it would.
'God was in control'.

I do not know what lies ahead
The way I cannot see;
Yet one stands near to be my guide,
He'll show the way to me;

I know who holds the future
And He'll guide me with His hand,
With God things don't just happen,
Everything by Him is planned;
So as I face tomorrow
With its problems large and small,
I'll trust the God of miracles
Give to Him my all

I do not know how many days
Of life are mine to spend;
But one who knows and cares for me
Will keep me to the end;

I know who holds the future........

I do not know the course ahead,
What joys and griefs are there;
But One is near who fully knows,
I'll trust His loving care;

I know who holds the future........

Gathering further experience

Now that I had visited St. Joseph's Hospice in Hackney, London, I continued my journey by visiting other hospices to get to know more about hospices, their environment, policies, criteria for admitting patients and the role of a 'Matron'.

My first call was to St. Francis in Romford which was in its infancy. I had an appointment with Dr. Kershaw who was a Trusteee of St. Francis.

He gave me a very warm welcome and patiently listened to "my story".

He was very sympathetic as, in those early days, he knew very well himself what was lacking and could understand my frustration at the lack of facilities for cancer patients in our area.

He was, of course, concerned about the financial implications. He felt if we were to go ahead, some of their supporters in the Thurrock area might want to support St. Luke's. This obviously would then be a financial loss to St. Francis Hospice. He reminded me of what it would involve and that it wouldn't all be "plain sailing", not the least financial, but encouraged me to go ahead as the population in both areas was too large to be served by only one hospice. Dr. Kershaw was very supportive and wished me all the best.

I also made an appointment with Fair Havens Hospice in Westcliffe and met their founder and Matron, Daphne Hall.

Daphne gave me a warm welcome, showed me around their hospice and we shared together some of our experiences.

We shared our concerns and hopes in prayer. To this day we remain great friends and continue to meet up at our "Matron's Munch" together with the retired Matron Janet, from Farleigh, Chelmsford and Jane, Director of Nursing from St Helena, Colchester.

The Matron from St. Luke's Hospice in Sheffield allowed me to shadow her for one week, again to gain more experience about a Matron's role and Hospice Management in general.

A further study weekend was spent there learning about the important task of the management of volunteers.

Hospices could not exist without the tremendous time volunteers give to the hospice.

At St. Christophers in London I met with Dame Cecily Saunders, founder of the modern hospice movement. Dame Cecily and her staff helped me and encouraged me greatly.

In fact, the wonderful way hospices work together and share their experience, their concerns and difficulties is quite unique.

Next on my list was Basildon Hospital where I met Richard, the Chief Executive. Richard kindly allowed me to contact the various deparments in his hospital to gain more experience and knowledge to help me in my future role as Matron.

My next call was Basildon Police Station. The police and the hospital gave me crash courses on staff management, employment laws and disciplinary issues. I tried to learn about as many aspects of management as I possibly could.

My thanks to all those wonderful people who helped me so much to gain knowledge and management skills as well as the support of the Royal College of Nurses and Midwives in London who would represent me should I meet any difficulties. The vision of a hospice was gaining momentum. My diary for these early months show meetings and conversations with doctors, bank manager, other hospices, Pastor John Turner, Mr Roy Ballentine from Basildon Hospital, and anyone who would listen.

Having received so much help and support from so many different people I promised myself that when the time came our hospice doors would always be open to help other professionals the same way as I had been helped.

Trudy's diary......

10 May
Tuesday

Dr. Dethams Surgery - handed over St. Lu
Dr. Maxwell   Hospice Noh

Bas. Hospital - Mr. Ballentine. Appt. 16,5

phoned
Charity Commission - are allowed to
collect money for St Lukes Hospice
but must not call it a Charity yet.

Registration will take 2-3 month

phoned Solicitor Brian Smith,
Will contact him again on Wednesday

May 6
St. Lukes Hospice.   Friday
Letter from Charity Commission arrived.
Colin Wind offered use of copying
machine as a contribution
Maureen Cavanagh from Marks -
Spencer phoned offering Ltd. Services +
½ Financial support.
8pm: meeting at Home
Yes + 3
Joan Maxwell
Allen Denham
Gerry Peaty
Mark Gallagher

Letter written by Trudy, dated 28th March 1983 to Mr M Gallagher FRICS, Principal Estates Officer, Basildon Development Corporation.

Dear Mr. Gallagher,

Further to our meeting of 11.3.83 may I prevail upon your kindness and patience and use this letter as a means of introducing myself, also to explain the main reasons for seeking your assistance in setting up a proposed Hospice within the Basildon area.

I am, as you are aware, a State Registered Nurse with a Queen's District Nursing Certificate.

I am married with three sons all brought up in Basildon. My family and I have lived in Basildon since 1961.

Since the early 60's I have worked as a District Nursing Sister for the community of Basildon.

Happy as I am with my association and nursing of the patients in the community - I am ever mindful of an urgent need for nursing the terminally ill.

I appreciate the support and facilities that the community have provided for the aged and infirmed, but as comprehensive as these facilities are, there is, I feel, a great need for some specialised care of the terminally ill, either at their home which can be distressing to their family or at a nursing home specially adapted for this patients care and need - a hospice, in fact.

On enquiring about the facilities available to help the terminally ill of Basildon and surrounding areas outside the general hospitals I have not been able to find a home purposefully adapted for their needs within Basildon.

It is this lack of a specialised home, plus the encouragement from colleagues, friends, church, general practitioners and many others that have prompted me to seek to rectify this lack of help for the terminally ill by attempting to gain a home adapted as a hospice.

There are, as I am aware, hospices being set up in the Southend, Chelmsford and Havering areas and doubtless other places in Essex but not in Basildon.

I need hardly tell you that, with the best motives in the world, I am not in a position to open a proposed hospice without you and other organised groups' and charities' assistance.

But we are willing to sell our house as a contribution and start in a small way and hopefully expand in phases as the need arises.

Attached to this letter is an appendix of people I have been in contact with who have given moral support and advice or who have pledged their support and help.

I offer this list as evidence of the encouragement and interest shown and the activities I have been engaged in since our last meeting.

The purpose of this letter is to ask for your help in achieving this aim of setting up a Hospice in Basildon.

You have already been very helpful and your continued advice would be gratefully received.

Yours faithfully, G. Cox.

Re: Registration of Hospice.

N.B. Reference to the application form sent by the Essex Area Health Authority I am at present unable to complete same as I do not have an official address for the proposed hospice.

Letter from Basildon Development Corporation, dated 6th April 1983 to Dr. R.T. Jones, Whitmorc Way, Basildon.

Dear Dr. Jones,

Nurse Cox - PRIVATE HOSPICE

Thank you for your letter of the 30th March, voicing your support for the idea of Nurse Cox for a private hospice in the town.

I agree with your sentiments that this would be a well needed facility in the Town and you may rest assured the Corporation will offer Nurse Cox every possible practical assistance.

The biggest obstacle from her point of view will obviously be the ability to raise the necessary finance for the running of such an operation. I think she will need all the help and expertise available to assist her in this aspect and, from the tone of your letter, I am confident that she will be able to count on the support of both yourself and your colleagues in the area.

There is the likelihood of a property becoming available in the vicinity of Basildon Hospital, which may prove ideal for this sort of purpose and, once it has been vacated, I will arrange for Mrs Cox to inspect the premises. I have also offered to attend any meetings that she may have with any possible financial backer, in order that I can explain the Corporation's position and the terms upon which the property is likely to be made available to her.

Yours sincerely, M. Gallagher, FRICS.
Principal Estates Officer.

BASILDON DEVELOPMENT CORPORATION

Gifford House, Basildon, Essex, SS13 2EX Tel: Basildon (0268) 553261 Answering Service after 5.15 p.m. Basildon (0268) 553377

Chief Estates Officer: D. J.E. Heard FRICS ARVA.

Our Ref: MG/EM. 22/62

Your Ref:

Ext:

Dr. R.T. Jones,
568 Whitmore Way,
Basildon,
Essex. SS14 2ER.

6th April, 1983

Dear Dr. Jones,

NURSE COX - PRIVATE HOSPICE

Thank you for your letter of the 30th March, voicing your support for the idea of Nurse Cox for a private hospice in the Town.

I agree with your sentiments that this would be a well needed facility in the Town and you may rest assured the Corporation will offer Nurse Cox every possible practical assistance.

The biggest obstacle from her point of view will obviously be the ability to raise the necessary finance for the running of such an operation. I think she will need all the help and expertise available to assist her in this aspect and from the tone of your letter, I am confident that she will be able to count on the support of both yourself and your colleagues in the area.

There is the likelihood of a property becoming available in the vicinity of Basildon Hospital, which may prove ideal for this sort of purpose and, once it has been vacated, I will arrange for Mrs Cox to inspect the premises. I have also offered to attend any meetings that she may have with any possible financial backer, in order that I can explain the Corporation's position and the terms upon which the property is likely to be made available to he

Yours sincerely,

M. GALLAGHER, FRICS.,
Principal Estates Officer.
MG/LT

Letter to Gladys

Dear Gladys,

I always mention you when talking about the story of St. Luke's. You, and your dear husband Tom, who always had a welcoming smile and the kettle on when I called on you all those years ago as your District Nurse.

You two were such a lovely contented couple and yet you were so ill! Housebound and unable to look after yourself, with your so swollen arm resting on the side of the armchair.

I can see you now, sitting there with your welcoming smile, never complaining, even if I was held up with another patient.

Tom sometimes looked so tired, but never admitting to it or complaining.

I so wanted to ease your burden, but all you could think of was how to help and support me in my endeavour to open a home to care for cancer patients and their families.

I always hoped that you would be our first day care patient. We could take care of you, share in any help and support you personally might need, and at the same time give Tom a 'day off' from caring for you.

But there was so much to think about, so much to plan, and where would the money come from?

But even in those early days we were able to help both you and Tom by starting a Sitting Service.

One of our dear volunteers would stay with you at home and Tom would be able to have a day to himself. He would be able to leave you for a few hours, doing what he wanted to do, with the knowledge that someone would take care of you, keep you company and share a few hours with you.

You, in fact, became our first Sitting Service patient.

The photograph was taken by Ron, a dear friend and supporter in those early days, with you and me smiling at each other, holding hands.

Roy, unbeknown to us both, took a close up of our hands and enlarged it.

Gladys - that famous photograph was used also on the front page of our Bereavement Leaflet and you and I, whenever we looked at it, giggled together and were so glad that our fingernails were clean.

So even in those difficult times we could laugh at such ordinary things as fingernails.

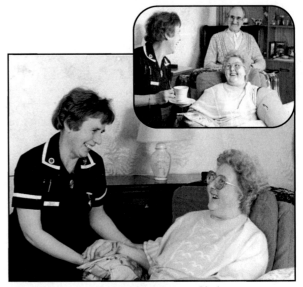

With my dear patient, Gladys

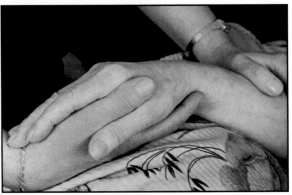

The Bereavement Leaflet hands

That photograph became the symbol of our Bereavement Service - by holding hands it symbolised the sharing with each other the sadness and heartache at the death of a loved one.

How strange life is, laughing one minute, sadness and tears the next, but we shared those precious moments together, you, Gladys, Tom and I.

I had always hoped that you would be our first day care patient but, sadly you didn't make it.

I want to thank you, Gladys, for allowing me to care for you, for allowing me to share with you my thoughts and hopes to care for cancer patients and their families, by allowing me to use that lovely photograph with you for our Sitting Service leaflet.

Thank you, Gladys, for helping me and for not only being my patient but for becoming a dear friend.

I miss you.

God bless.

Trudy

Meeting Estate Agents

A few days after that special Christmas I was called to visit a new patient.

He was curled up at the bottom of his bed crying out in pain begging me, 'Sister, Sister, put me down - you wouldn't let an animal suffer like this!'

I was so distressed. Thankfully, I managed to contact an emergency doctor who helped to ease the patient's pain and I was then able to make him comfortable.

The suffering of this patient, whom I was privileged to nurse, together with the experience of that Christmas Eve and the little children, really confirmed my resolve now that I just had to open a Home for Cancer Patients.

The situation with my patient affected me so much that I felt I had to put my thoughts and experiences down on paper. Not for anyone in particular but mainly, I suppose, for me. Writing about all the feelings I was going through was a form of release to the burden I was carrying at that time.

Billericay High St. today, with the old Health Authority building

After a few days I went back to see my patient. He felt much better and we were able to walk in his garden. He could see how upset I had been and I told him how my visit to him had made me sit down and write down my thoughts. He then asked to see what I had written.

I was able to share with my patient my nursing experiences with patients like himself, without mentioning any names, and my resolve to open a home for cancer patients. He told me I had to do it and again said to me - 'Sister, no one should have to suffer like I did'. I have never forgotten his words to me on that day.

This dear patient lived for another three weeks and eventually died peacefully at home.

On my next day off I happened to be in Billericay, walking down the High Street.

As I looked up, I saw an estate agents office and thought it can't hurt to go in and find out if there were any suitable premises to open a home for cancer patients.

How naïve, thinking they would help!

When the agent heard that all I had was 25p he quickly showed me the door. Well, I was silly thinking I could get a house for 25p. But, as God would have it, there was another estate agent's office a few doors along. I got all my courage together with a 'help me look' to heaven and boldly walked in. He was very helpful in telling me that he was sure he could find something suitable but quickly changed his mind when he saw my 25p and politely showed me the door.

Well, what did I expect? A house for 25p. Thinking about it, I couldn't even blame him. Fancy thinking I could get a house for 25p!

Even now, writing this, I feel still embarrassed. Who on earth would give a house for 25p? Despondent, I walked to my car but, before reaching it, I saw a third estate agent's premises.

But courage failed me. Having been shown the door twice how could I possible think of going to try again?

Meeting Malcolm and Mark

All my belief suddenly came flooding back. Someone has just got to help. At the same time I felt so embarrassed. I simply couldn't go in until in my head, I saw John, a young very sick patient of mine, and then I decided, all good things come in threes and with John in my head and a 'please God help me' prayer, I walked in before I could change my mind. A nice young man greeted me and asked if he could help.

Without hesitation I said 'I do hope so, but I only have 25p, but I would very much appreciate it if you could spare a little time and listen to me and if you than want to throw me out, I will just go away'.

But, bless him, he allowed me to unburden myself. Without mentioning names, I told him about some of my patients, and their desperate needs.

He listened intently and patiently and then, 'God bless him always' He said he felt sure that he could help.

He said he would get in touch with the Council and Basildon Corporation to see if there was anything that could be done.

I could have hugged him. He was so interested and could see how desperate I was. He took my details and thanking him profusely, I went on my way home, very happy. At least there was someone who had listened, was so encouraging, and hopeful.

Still today I thank God for that lovely young man and only wish I could remember his name.

How I would love to tell him that with his help and support and his believing in the project, today St. Luke's Hospice is here - giving love, support and help to many people and their families in their hour of need.

As I arrived home, the telephone was ringing. It was my young friend from the estate agent.

For a split second I thought he had changed his mind but he apologised for disturbing me and said he just needed to know my qualifications.

He said in all the excitement he forgot to ask. I was able to reassure him that I had my nursing qualifications with certificates to prove it.

That evening I told Les about the visits to the estate agents and about my new friend.

A few days later, I had another call from my estate agent. He told me that he had been in touch with the

Malcolm and Mark

then Basildon Corporation and had arranged a meeting with them and me at their Planning Department in Basildon.

I, happily and with great anticipation, went with him to meet Mark and Malcolm, two young men who were from the Planning Department. They told me that they were planning a new estate (now known as Noak Hill Estate) and maybe a purpose built building would be appropriate for our needs.

I was very excited and thought how generous they were suggesting that, and being me and very spontaneous with a picture mind, I saw a beautiful building in my head. Little did I know that my estate agent friend hadn't told them that all I had was 25p.

When I dropped that bombshell, they were both speechless for a moment and just couldn't believe what they had just heard.

I felt again very naïve and silly thinking I could get a house for 25p but at the same time I could not help thinking that it should be possible.

I mentioned to them that there were many nice and big empty houses that were vacated through compulsory purchase order but not yet used for whatever they planned to do with them.

Could I in the meantime have one of those houses? Get friends and family together to help with preparing them, painting and decorating, clearing parking space and put the house to good use? If they needed it back, maybe there would be another one available?

They just looked at me in disbelief and suggested a good strong cup of coffee might be in order.

Meeting Harry Bacon

I then told them about my patient who died on Christmas Eve, alone and without help, surrounded by her children who thought she was just asleep. Thinking back to that Christmas I felt strongly that if we had had a house then I could have done the nursing, maybe one or two of my friends could have helped with taking the children to school and the cooking and laundering. It all sounded so simple and yet seemed so difficult.

Both Mark and Malcolm had a little chat between them and then told me we could not have a purpose built building because it would be too expensive but there was a farm house that might be suitable.

I got so excited but they calmed me down and said that they would have to speak with their Chief Executive and see if that was possible.

At this time they couldn't tell me where the farmhouse was and said I just had to be patient and that they would get in touch with me.

Now, trying to be patient and not to be excited but hopeful was very difficult for me but I just knew in my heart, that God meant for Les and me to help those dear patients of mine and that something was about to happen.

Harry Bacon

The telephone call came some time later for me to go and meet their boss. I was so hopeful and yet also very nervous and scared. A house for 25p? Who would be so generous to help us?.

I will never forget my first visit to the Corporation for my meeting with Mark and Malcolm's Chief Executive, Harry Bacon. Harry, newly promoted to Chief Executive, had worked previously for the London County Council before joining Basildon Development Corporation in 1961. Never in my whole life had I been in a boardroom, and yet, there he was, this very important man and I, a little scared District Nurse, who felt too afraid to enter the room.

Then I quickly put my patient 'Gladys' in my picture head and said to her that I will go in and tell him about her and patients like her.

I entered and Harry looked to me a bit fearsome, but was very kind. Again I told him that I so desperately wanted to help my patients by providing a home for them where their needs could be met and to help ease their pain and support them at a very difficult time in their life as well as their families.

Patiently Harry listened and then told me about the farmhouse, suggesting I go and see it.

If I thought it was suitable I was to get back to him. I was not to mention the site or the house to anyone. I was so excited and hopeful I went to see this special house as soon as I could.

There I was, all by myself, looking at the old farmhouse, the scullery, the pig sty and the long grass around me.

Fobbing Farm and outbuildings

It was very quiet apart from the sound of the traffic noise.

I looked at the hospital and college in the distance and just stood there, looking back at the old farmhouse.

Then, in the quiet of the moment, I heard very clearly God's voice:......'The ground you are standing on is holy ground' (Exodus3 v 5) I remember saying,, 'pardon' and looking around and up but no one was there. I was alone.

But I clearly felt God's presence, never before or since in my Christian journey did I feel God's spirit so close to me. From that moment ... I just knew that's where our new home for our patients had to be.

Since that early meeting Harry and I have become great friends.

Forming A Management Committee

My next concern was to get the right people to join the Management Committee.

As God had called us to this work, we were anxious that like-minded people would join us; people who knew that God was on our side, would together pray for guidance, for health and strength, for the right way to go forward.

```
Clear our thoughts
Save us from useless talk,
And grant us a sober view of ourselves:
To see our possibilities and limitations.
Not to be proud of our successes
Nor to despair over our failures.

Help us to realise that we have no right
To excuse ourselves with our impotence before you
Neither boast with our abilities in your sight.

Grant us understanding among ourselves:
May we never hurriedly harmonise
Where we genuinely disagree,
Nor quarrel over anything less important than the truth.
Teach us loving trust for each other.

Lord, we pray: Let your spirit guide us tonight.
```

I felt it was important to have a doctor with us, a sympathetic and committed person, a person we felt comfortable with and who was as anxious as we were to help our patients.

How to find that special person?

It didn't take long. I was nursing a very sick patient at the time at home, who was in great pain and needed three hourly injections which involved night time visits.

I managed to get a Marie Curie nurse to come during the night, but one evening at 5pm, I found out I could not have them any longer. I was told that I was on call and that I should deal with it.

I was stunned and could not believe it! For the first time ever, and since, I lost it. I feel ashamed now for shouting at my nurse manager that he could not do that and that the patient needed her injections. I just could not believe what I was hearing. He told me the money allocated to that particular patient had run out. I asked why I wasn't told before.

I knew the Marie Curie Foundation would be very upset about this, as they were established to help out in these situations but it did no good.

He said that there was no money and no Marie Curie nurse. I just hung up. I knew I could not work day and night, so what now?

Distressed, and in tears of frustration, I went to see Jean, the GP who was responsible for that particular patient.

Jean felt just the same as I did. So we both decided to take it in turns to do the night injections.

Jean did it without hesitation and I felt a doctor who would be that kind and passionate would be just the person we needed.

I asked Jean and she agreed to come on the Management Committee. So now we were three - Les, myself and Jean.

Edna was a colleague of mine on 'the district'. Mature and wise, a committed Christian, very kind and very correct in all she did. We got on well together.

Edna was just the person we needed. She shared my concerns for patients but was not as emotional as I am and therefore was a good balance which was so important.

We all had different gifts and Edna was our gift of wisdom, as we lovingly called it. Thus Edna became a member of the Management Committee.

Jenni was a student nurse at Basildon Hospital. From time to time, we, as District Nursing Sisters were required to take students on our 'rounds'.

It was part of their training to familiarise them with how patients were cared for in their own homes in the community.

Jenni and I soon became friends. She also was committed to the best care possible for the patients, at the same time not forgetting the family. Jenni had many questions to ask me and kept me on my toes.

I soon realised how clever she was, very articulate and clever in putting pen to paper. She also had a great gift of communicating with patients and family members, which is obviously necessary.

Needless to say I asked Jenni if she would join us at the Management Committee which she prayerfully agreed.

Our First Management Committee

Our first Management Committee

As in any organisation we needed someone with secretarial gifts, someone who could record the minutes of our meetings and who else but Pat? Pat was a secretary at our Vange Health Centre, which was the base for us District Nurses.

Pat and I always got on well. We had the same joy of living, and sense of humour, but she shared with me many a time when I was distressed at what was happening and was often a great comfort to me.

She knew how I felt and she was eager to help. So Pat became and was our Secretary for many years.

Through Jean we were introduced to Ruth and Gerry, who both were members of Jean's church. We all became friends instantly.

Ruth became involved with fundraising and giving talks to share the vision of St. Luke's and Gerry, a Chartered Accountant, became our treasurer.

The Management Committee was complete.

Thank you, God.

Jean

Edna

Jenni

Pat

Gerry

Les

Trudy

Ruth

First Management Committee

Les	-	Administrator	Gerry	-	Accountant
Jean	-	Doctor	Trudy	-	Matron
Edna	-	District Nurse	Jenni	-	Nurse
Ruth	-	Fundraiser	Pat	-	Secretary

First Public Meetings In Vange And Billericay

Our first public meeting took place at the Vange Health Centre, Clay Hill Road, Basildon.

Since I first announced my vision of opening a hospice for cancer patients, I had started to talk about it and involve my nursing colleagues, friends and family. It obviously had created a great deal of interest.

The first interview (by a very nervous Jean and Trudy) at Fobbing Farm

First public meeting in Vange Health Centre

We (the Management Committee) and all our helpers felt the best way to explain all about the hospice for cancer patients was to hold a public meeting.

Having decided that, it then turned out to be a very difficult meeting in answering some of the questions. We were not yet free to disclose the site of the future hospice. We were not yet allowed to officially fundraise, We couldn't explain the shape of the building, and so on.... So why, you may ask, did we decide to hold a public meeting?

First public meeting in the Archer Hall, Billericay

The reason was that we were getting so many enquiries all the time about the proposed project that we felt the time was right. It was definitely easier to share in this way with friends in our community the happenings and the vision and hope for the hospice for cancer patients and their families and why there was a need for this important service and to explain the support and encouragement we had so far.

Then, inevitably, the question of finance came up. I always tried to answer truthfully. "I don't know how," I said, "but I know we will do it. With God's and everyone's help, it will happen."

Billericay residents met a charity teams at the town's Archer Hall on Monday to discuss the St Luke's Hospice Appeal. St Luke's representatives invited townspeople to the meeting to find out more about the charity project. The hospice, at which terminally ill people will be cared for, is to be set up at the Fobbing Farmhouse in Nethermayne, Basildon. The plans include a £240,000 purpose-built extension. Pictured at Monday's meeting are members of the hospice management committee, from left (back row) Mrs Pat Frisby, Mrs Ruth Booth, and Mr Gerald Peaty, (front row) Mrs Trudi Cox, Dr Jean Maxwell and Mrs Edna Blakeman.

Hospice appeal

A MEETING aimed boosting the St Luke's Hospice appeal is to be held Billericay's Archer Hall February 11.

St Luke's representat are inviting Billeri people to the meeting find out more about charity project.

The plans for the hosp are centred on the Fobb farmhouse in Nethermay Basildon, with a £240, purpose-built extension.

Terminally ill peo would be cared for at

Terminally ill people would be cared for at the hospice.

Mrs Ruth Booth, a member of the hospice council of management, said: "Our aim is to invite local business and professional people to come and find out more about the project.

"Our appeal is going very well and we have received help from many local organisations and individuals.

"However, we feel that many more people could assist us in this work if they knew more about it," she said.

The meeting starts at 6pm.

How the newspapers reported the first public meeting in Billericay's Archer Hall, one year into the vision of a local Hospice

"God works through people, so you see, we need your support in whichever way you can. By giving us some of your time, helping with fundraising, your talents are needed - financial and prayerful support."

More public meetings were held. Our local police force kindly allowed us to use their conference room to talk about hospice work and all it entails and to show a video: "Help the Hospice." Afterwards we were invited for a drink in the social club - which was enjoyed by us all.

Management Committee and Cox Family visit Fobbing Farm for the first time

......and in we go

Naturally everyone was delighted to find that the farm contains a luxurious bathroom suite !

The shiny new kitchen area more than makes up for any other shortcomings !

Not to be outdone, the downstairs toilet offered a similar superior convenience !

Our first visit to Fobbing Farm - 'The House on the Hill' that was later to become St. Luke''s Hospice - was very exciting.   Expectantly we gathered and I turned the large old key in the lock.

With little Christopher peeping over my shoulder. Gerry, Judy, Keith and Edna, with Jean and her little dog following, we entered the old farmhouse kitchen.

Christopher was allowed to enter first and choose his bedroom, and as expected, he chose the largest room upstairs so that his snooker table would fit.

Les, Christopher and I had to adapt ourselves to living in a flat.

The photographs show a little part of the inside of the old farmhouse.

The words sum up our first impressions of what it wouldill be like to live in our new home.

The flat would be our home for the next six years.

The Committee inspects Fobbing Farm

Next followed an informal tour of the grounds and building exterior by the Committee and the Cox family.

Fobbing Farm actually dates from the turn of the century - the 1900s that is. The red bricked annexe was added at a later date and, although it added character to the house, the brickwork was flaky and crumbled to the touch.

There were two annexes - one in front of the kitchen, the other on the grounds. Both had to be removed.

There then followed a crash course in site construction. I quickly learned all about main drainage, sewers and cess pools.

"What is a cess pool?" I asked and everyone laughed. We also would need all the main utilities, i.e., gas, electricity and water, renewed and connected again.

Well, what do you think is down there ?
No prizes for guessing what everyone is wishing for!

Hmm... I think the first thing we need to get is a rake and a skip !

Christopher having a well earned rest from talk of Fobbing Farm

Front elevation showing the piggery

Front door steps which prompted Les to blandly remark "of course the steps will need sweeping".

20

Training of Volunteers, Cancer Care and Bereavement Support and Sitting Service

Training of Volunteers.

While we were waiting for the Charity Commission to give us our charity number and, with that, permission to fundraise, there were many other things we could do to help my patients and their families in the meantime.

It was very obvious that we needed more helpers, volunteers who would freely give their time, talents, love and support.

With the help of my friends from Social Services, nursing friends and secretaries from the local Health Centre, we started the training scheme for volunteers.

Of course, we hadn't any money to pay for teaching premises. We were so fortunate that churches, clubs and schools allowed us to use their halls free of charge for the training of our future volunteers.

Volunteer training courses continue to this day with many people still coming forward; the young and not so young - after all these years it is truly amazing.

Cancer Care and Family Support.

Time was always my biggest enemy. There was so much to do. Patients and their families not only needed nursing care, they also needed time spent with them to support them in other ways.

So, once a month, helped by our volunteers, we would organise an evening at our home in Clay Hill Road to support cancer patients and their families.

This was an opportunity for them to share with us and each other all their concerns, their despair at times, their isolation and helplessness in the new situation they found themselves in.

The Sitting Service.

Another concern we had was the need to provide a form of help for the carers and families of patients in their own homes. Once we had completed our first volunteer course we began to interview volunteers for this important role. They would have to be suitable and willing to sit with a patient at home. Carers suffer almost as much as the patient as they watch their loved ones in pain, in distress and fear, not knowing what to do. Often carers are tired and exhausted themselves but soldier on the best they know how.

Our Sitting Service would give the carers of the patient - many of whom would have spent all day and many hours in the night caring for their loved ones - an opportunity to have a few hours to look after themselves. They badly needed a little time on their own to recharge their batteries. So we established The Sitting Service.

Bereavement Support Service.

As District Nurses we always had new patients, new referrals and new visits to make. It was obvious that time would not allow us to continue to visit the families of patients who had died. Usually we did just one follow up visit to make sure they were 'ok' But, of course, they were not.

Their life was now completely turned upside-down and nothing would ever be the same again for them, After that one follow up visit I always felt bad. I had the feeling I was virtually leaving the family high and dry.

Once the patient had died my nursing duties had ended - full stop. But I knew these families needed continued support. Their very busy lives had been changed and now they had time on their hands. They would experience utter loneliness, sadness, hopelessness and despair.

They desperately needed someone to talk and to listen. Listening was the biggest gift we could give to them. With these thoughts in mind we began inviting bereaved families into our home to spend time with us on another evening a month.

My nursing friends, social services colleagues and secretaries from the local Health Centre again helped me. Here the families could share their need and sadness as well as gaining support from other bereaved families.

Out of these monthly meetings grew what became known as our Bereavement Support Service.

The Charity Commission and First Visit to the Bank

Having never done any charity work I had no idea of the protocol and security checks. All I knew was that I needed a Charity Number in order to be legally allowed to fundraise. One thing I also knew was that we needed was money and lots of it.

So one day I just telephoned the Charity Commission. I told them who I was and what I wanted to do and would they be so kind and send me a Charity Number.

There was a long silence. I must have been the only person in the country who was so naïve as to think you just phone and, hey presto, a Charity Number, is given to you.

After a pause, which seemed endless. The voice at the other end of the telephone replied to tell me that they can't just give me a number but they would send me some information.

Soon following that first telephone call to the Charity Commission a parcel arrived with a letter explaining that the first thing I needed to do is employ a solicitor!

What with? We had no money, and who would want to help us free of charge??.

Do solicitors do that? I think it was Gerry who came to the rescue.

He knew a Christian Solicitor who might be interested in helping us. We, the Committee Members - were introduced to Brian, who couldn't give his service free, but would help us with a reduced fee.

We agreed thankfully and so the process of registering as a charity began in earnest.

In the meantime I contacted the Charity Commission again. I explained that I understood that I couldn't ask for money but there were people who wanted to give me a donation and I really didn't want to refuse it.

Could I not accept it as long as it was given freely, without my asking? They agreed, but made me aware of being very careful — accurate accounting was the order of the day.

I will be ever grateful for them for their advice and I duly decided to set up a charity account with Nat West Bank. Our family account was with Barclays Bank.

It is a great responsibility being trusted with public money and we were fully aware of this.

Following my telephone call to the Charity Commission I arrived one afternoon at the Nat West Bank counter with our very first donation.

St Andrews Church Ladies had collected loose change and presented me with a very heavy biscuit tin full of money.

The time was 3.20pm.

The lady behind the counter wasn't too pleased to be asked to open an account for me at such a late hour and gave me the appropriate sigh and look to teach me better banking times.

She looked really exasperated as I opened my precious biscuit tin and let all the pennies and halfpennies roll into the tray,

"Haven't you bagged it?" she asked me sternly?

Well, I didn't know what bagging was, so she showed me lots of little plastic bags with various denominations written on it, pushed them in a cloth bag and instructed me to use them in future.

While she counted those (to me) precious pennies, a young man arrived with forms to help me with the paperwork.

Charity Number and Collecting Boxes

'Name of Charity?' he asked and couldn't believe me when I had to tell him that we hadn't got an official name.

I couldn't think so quickly and also knew it wasn't my decision alone to name the charity so I quickly told him to call it 'Trudy's Charity', for the time being.

There was great excitement at our next committee meeting when we received the wonderful news.

We had been granted our official charity number

2 8 9 4 6 6

How grateful we were and we thanked God for the wonderful news - asking Him for guidance and wisdom.

The name 'Trudy's Charity' stayed with us until approximately a year later when, at a meeting with our Management Committee, it was decided to choose the name 'St. Luke's Hospice.'

Having received permission from the Charity Commission and our charity number we were now ready to commence fundraising in earnest. Not with biscuit tins, of course. We needed official collecting boxes - it was a legal requirement, too.

We didn't, at that time, have any money to buy them so I needed someone to make them free of charge. I approached Bader House in Basildon which was a building training centre for people with physical disabilities.

I always remember our first official fundraising boxes, little wooden boxes made and nailed together by our friends at Bader House.

They worked so hard and we in turn then distributed these precious boxes amongst families and friends.

Since then these early boxes have been replaced by our red 'official collection boxes' with our charity number and hospice details printed on them.

Now it was 'all systems go' on our fundraising.

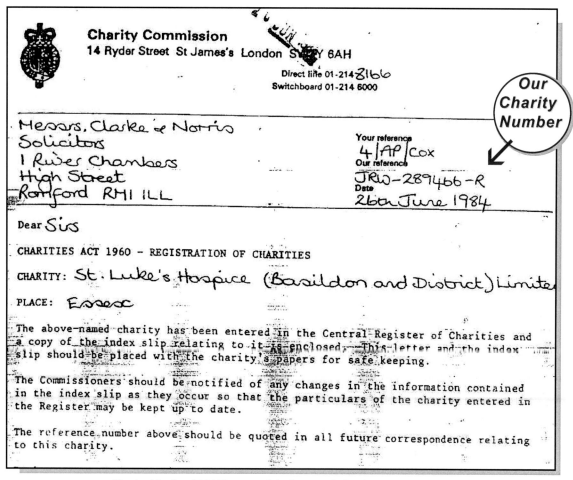

Charity Number 289466 - part of the letter with the all important charity number

Charity Number and Collecting Boxes

With the permission of the Councils in both the Thurrock and Basildon areas, we were allowed to have official street collections by our dedicated fundraisers.

We were able to put the boxes into shops, factories and businesses. And, of course, wherever there is a hospice function, or at presentations and talks, the red boxes are always with us.

Jean, Ruth, Edna and I continued giving talks and spreading the good news about St. Luke's and through these public meetings, more donations were received.

A collection of collecting boxes

We now have little yellow hospice boxes for loose change. It's amazing how pennies become pounds whenever we empty our pockets and purses into a yellow hospice box. Our loose change boxes can be picked up at the Hospice if you would like to help us.

Why 'Luke'

I am often asked why we chose the name of Luke for the hospice. The apostle Luke was a well loved physician, kind, sympathetic but, at the same time, a very learned man. He followed Jesus in his teachings, a man with love in action and that's what we wanted to do also.

The management committee are committed Christians and Luke, from the New Testament, was not only a physician, a doctor with knowledge and compassion, but also a very sensitive, kind man who told us in the New Testament about Jesus, and his love for his people.

Luke, we are told, may have met Jesus but, if not, almost certainly met people who had had contact with Jesus.

We felt that if we could live like Jesus wanted us to live, by loving those in need of love, help and support, that is what we should strive to do.

So after praying about choosing the name for the hospice we decided on St. Luke's.

The Shield -- our emblem

It was Les who suggested the shield.

In the New Testament in Ephesians 6 it talks about the armour of God, the belt of truth, the breastplate of rightousness, the shield of faith and the power of prayer.

The story about St. Luke's is all about faith in God and his people.

> *The Armour of God*
>
> [10]Finally, be strong in the Lord and in his mighty power. [11]Put on the full armour of God so that you can take your stand against the devil's schemes. [12]For our struggle is not against flesh and blood, but against the rulers, against the authorities, against the powers of this dark world and against the spiritual forces of evil in the heavenly realms. [13]Therefore put on the full armour of God, so that when the day of evil comes, you may be able to stand your ground, and after you have done everything, to stand.

The House On The Hill

On another visit to the House on the Hill, again I felt so at peace and although God didn't 'speak' to me this time, I knew that it was His will that this lovely house should become our hospice.

How happy I was when I left the 'House on the Hill' now known as St. Luke's Hospice.

It really was ideally situated, a little set aside on a hill and a neighbour to the College and Sports Centre, so the patients could hear and see children.

Basildon Hospital was just a few yards further. I could ask doctors to come across and help instead of dragging patients to the hospital.

In the distance could be heard the sound of traffic. Again, that was good for the patients could watch the world go by but, with double glazing,, nothing would disturb them.

So, the patients would be surrounded by daily noises and sounds which is important. A dying patient is still a living patient' who need the sounds of life around them.

Our photos show the moment when the "Certificate of Incorporation of a private limited company" was signed by Jean and Edna. This effectively meant that we were now a company limited by guarantee, registration number: 1812104. A happy Gerry is holding the signed Certificate of Incorporation.

With renewed enthusiasm and the knowledge and confirmation that God is on our side, I revisited Harry, the Chief Executive of the Basildon Corporation and shared with him my experience at the House on the Hill.

Harry informed me the Members of the Corporation had had a meeting and, to make the proposed rental of the 'House' legal, they felt a peppercorn rent would be appropriate.

(In all honesty I can't remember the exact figure of the rent. It may have been £5 or £50 but, in reality, we never actually paid the rent. Someone kindly made the payment for us through a donation)

Further meetings followed between our Management Committee and Harry - Chief Executive, of Basildon Corporation (later known as the Commission for the New Town).

The next step would be signing the lease for Fobbing Farm and eventually we signed the freehold for the building which was now to be known as 'St. Luke's Hospice'.

Fundraising
and Fundraisers

As you read through this book you will meet time and again stories of the many wonderful people who helped build St. Luke's in a fundraising sense.

Looking through my volumes of photographs and newspaper cuttings, I have selected these at random to give you, the reader, a flavour of the great support St. Luke's received.

I hope those I have missed will forgive me. We received great support from many businesses, factories, social clubs, football teams, and many different organisations and, of course, the many individuals who helped us.

I could write another book just on fundraising and fundraisers and their stories of kindness, love and support for our vision of a hospice.

I am always amazed when hearing about the ingenuity of so many people to think up so many different ideas to raise money for St. Luke's. Not only the planned events but the spontaneous ones, too and, of course, their committment and tenacity to encourage family and friends and the general public to support them.

As you will see, this support came not only from our own locality but was on a world wide scale.

Without all of you St. Luke's would not have happened.

I am so grateful to everyone who helped us.

Thank you.

I would like to add that the following pages are my personal recollection of events and my memories. Please forgive me if I have got things wrong or made errors in the telling of the Hospice story. I have tried to remember things accurately and have checked certain details with friends and those involved in the story of the Hospice.

Co-founder & Patron,
St. Luke's

Who Could Help Us ?

Then came the question, 'Who could help us?'

We had many friends, family, kind neighbours, colleagues who following the meeting in our house showed enthusiasm and support.

I thought about our community at large - what makes a community?. Who are they ?

Here we were, living in a new town of Basildon but where were all the people who could help us? We badly needed financial and all kinds of support.

I made a list of the Health Authority covering all the areas in Thurrock, Basildon, Billericay and Wickford . I also compiled a list of all the various organisations in our area.

Thurrock Council	Our MPs
Basildon Council	Rotary
Basildon Hospital	Lions
Education Deptartment.	40 club
Social Services	Inner Wheel
Schools and Nurseries	Stores and Shops
Churches	M. & S.
Colleges	Woolworth
Voluntary Agencies	W H Smith
Police	Department Stores
Fire	Banks
Chemists	Ambulance
Newspaper Shops	Factories

Once I had written a list, the next step was to visit these organisations and ask for their help and support.

Practical ! Financial ! and Prayerful !.

I started at the top - as I knew if I went to middle management it would be a chain of managers before I would reach the person who could make final decisions.

My first call was Basildon Hospital. I made an appointment to see the Chief Executive and was granted an interview.

Thus I met Richard Taylor, who showed great patience by listening to my story. He also felt that there was a need to help these dear people suffering from cancer and promised to assist in any way he could.

Through Richard I was then able to meet with other hospital managers from whom I gained advice on general management, health and safety and other important issues.

Our local GPs in surgeries and Health Centres were very interested and promised to support where needed.

Visiting my chemist one day I met two police officers.

They encouraged me to see their Chief Commander. I duly made an appointment and met Alan Gilling, who became a great support and help to us.

Standing next to the Police Station were our Ambulance and Fire Service Premises. I duly introduced myself, told my story and both promised to become part of the Community Services supporting our cause.

Next on my list were our Councillors, Members of Parliament, the Education Authority, Social Services and then the numerous organisations: The Lions, Round Table, Rotary and Inner Wheel, Guilds, local Social Groups and of course our local shops, from Marks & Spencer, W H Smith, Woolworths and the surrounding stores.

I visited vicars/ministers of our local churches, gave talks at the various meetings, made friends with Sunday School children, with the Cubs, Brownies, Scout and Guide movements. Various other social centres joined in in making various items for sale.

The momentum was amazing; so many people felt that there was a great need for facilities to help cancer patients and their families. More and more people and organisations joined us. It was wonderful and so reassuring.

Local radio stations joined in and I had my first radio interview with Roy Smith, the local radio presenter. I was so very nervous but somehow I managed to carry on. He invited us for a further interview which Jean and I nervously attended. We were good together - helping each other out when one of us was lost for words.

Helpers Coming Forward

During all this time of preparation, planning and meetings - many people came forward to give their support in any way they could.

We never wanted to lose sight that it was God's work we were doing.

My photograph shows one of our early prayer groups who met regularly to support us in this way.

My friends from the German Lutheran Church did a spontaneous collection after listening to 'my story' so it wasn't only in Thurrock and Basildon that people were raising money for the building of St. Luke's.

If you will forgive a little bit of family indulgence, the following photographs will explain an international flavour to our fundraising.

My parents held a prayer meeting their own home in Germany for the hospice. An instant collection was

taken to raise funds for St. Luke's.

My brother Gerold, working in Tripoli, did the same in his United Church there.

It was truly a form of Worldwide Help.

Marks of friendship

Brotherly love helps hospice

A SPECIAL gift from strife-torn Libya to Basildon's St Lukes Hospice has reunited a brother and sister, and proved charity knows no boundaries.

Matron Trudy Cox, 48, received the $1,000 cheque from her engineer brother, Gerold Muller, who works in the Libyan capital Tripoli.

The money was raised by people of all nationalities at the Union Church of Tripoli, and without knowing of Gerold's family connection with the hospice, members wanted to help.

This was the third donation from the church, but this time Gerold, 50, who is church chairman, was able to deliver the money personally to his sister because he was in Britain on a study trip.

More Helpers, young and old, came forward to help

No matter how little is donated, like a little acorn, it will grow into a beautiful tree or, as in our case, a place where cancer patients and their families will find love, hope, compassion and help.

The letter on this page was received from the Senior Citizens Club of Whitmore Way Community Centre.

We need the little donations like this. Believe me, they grow and help us to continue this valuable work.

Another senior citizen, 94 year old Mrs Tingle, celebrated her birthday by asking for a donation for the hospice instead of birthday presents.

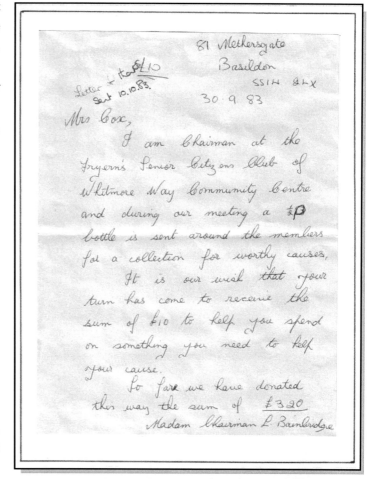

Our two young supporters wanted to have a sale to raise money for St. Luke's. They made up the brightly coloured banners to attract the customers to buy their unwanted toys.

Barry and Terry from Billericay invited us to an auction in their garden. As well as items to bid for they sold plants and provided refreshments and music too. It was exciting to watch the thermometer climb as the bidding heated up and the donations for the hospice grew.

Our Fundraising Canoeists Save A Life

Toni and Frank heard about the planned hospice and decided to do a sponsored canoe paddle the length of the river Thames. They raised £1,600 for St. Luke's Hospice.

They set off from Lechlade in Gloucestershire for their 200 mile paddle.

We met them on their second night stop where we learned their story of how they had saved a man's life.

On their first day they had spotted a jogger collapsed on the river bank. They quickly paddled to the side of the river and leapt out.

In no time Frank, a qualified life saver, was giving the victim the kiss of life. The jogger had suffered a heart attack.

While Frank was busy with the victim, Toni ran back along the tow path to the nearest telephone a few miles away to call for an ambulance.

Thanks to their quick thinking the man was taken to hospital where he made a full recovery. Toni and Frank continued with their paddling !

Well done, Toni and Frank.

River rescue drama

Canoe pair save heart attack man

TWO men canoeing down the Thames for Basildon Hospice saved a jogger's life.

Frank Palmer, of Laburnum Drive, Corringham, and Tony Cox, of Foxhunter Walk, Billericay, were mooring their canoes when Frank saw a jogger on the bank keel over.

His wife Kathy said Frank saw the man suffer a heart attack.

She said: "Frank rushed over and caught him as he was slipping down the bank.

"He started to give the kiss of life while Tony made for the phone.

"It turned out the nearest phone was in a pub nearly five miles away and Tony ran all the way.

"By the time the ambulance arrived about three-quarters of

Another one of our adventurous fundraisers, was Peter Kavanagh.

In 1992 Peter took on the arduous 190 mile Coast to Coast walk through Cumbria and into Yorkshire.

Setting off from St Bee's Head on the Irish coast Peter walked all the way to Scarborough to raise money for the hospice.

Peter's parents Maureen and Peter Kavanagh senior, have been supporters of St. Luke's since the very beginning, Their son, Peter, was sadly a victim in the Southall train crash tragedy.

Our Early Fundraising

From the vision of the hospice, throughout its preparation, following completion of the building, from the moment the first patient arrived and to the present day, everyone had to work very hard to make sure the necessary funds were available.

Fundraising is one of the most important aspects of hospice life as, without the money being raised, we would not be able to carry out the work we have been called to do.

I asked God to help us daily, first in raising the necessary funds and then to help give us the wisdom to use it wisely.

The responsibility of using public funds is great and all of us are fully aware of that.

I never will be able to thank God enough for all the wonderful people who so faithfully helped us, and are still helping in raising the necessary funds A great big **THANK YOU** to you all.

I remember with great affection our very first fundraising efforts:

Friends and I would meet outside our family home in Clay Hill Road. Bric a Brac would be left outside my front door.

One of our hospice friends would arrive in

a white van to collect it all up and take it off to sell in the Flea Market in Basildon Town Centre.

During this time, our house in Clay Hill Road became the official venue for our committee meetings as well as storage for donated items.

Our garage and part of our home gradually filled with bric a brac and donated items.

Often, on coming home from my visits as a District Nurse, I had to park the car across the road.

The driveway and front garden of our house were filled with all sorts of items.

I remember the fun we had.

It became a very familiar sight to see Peggy, Margaret, and Doris push the pram full of donated items, come rain or come shine, or snow, to Fryerns Community Hall for our first jumble and bric-a-brac sales.

In those early days tin foil, milk bottle tops and Meals on Wheel containers were also collected.

Once a week you would find Hilda and Connie (from Fryerns church) sitting in our loft separating tin foil.

Peggy, Margaret, Doris and me loading up the fundraising pram

Whenever I had a moment I would join in the fun! We had to spray the house with air fresheners, as the smell of sour milk bottle tops and left-over bits from those meals filled the house. Hilda and Connie certainly were my heroes.

Once sorted, I took the filled sacks in our van to Laindon for recycling, coming home with my 'pay' for the hospice.

That's how the early money was raised for the hospice.

Our loft became our 'store cupboard'

Connie and Hilda sorting bottle tops

Skipping Kelly and Paddling Bill

Active fundraising continued. Volunteers who had been with us from the early days continued working hard while, at the same time, new people joined us, young and old. I had no idea that we had so many kind, helpful, gifted people among us and some as young as only five years old.

When I was working as a District Nurse I had the privilege of caring for one little girl's grandfather.

Her name was Kelly and when she heard about the planned hospice and that we were trying to raise the necessary funds she wanted to help.

Kelly told me; "It's a place to make people better and if it can't they go to Jesus in heaven. He is looking after my grandad'

Then Kelly thought of a great fundraising idea.

She would do a sponsored skip for us - and she did! Kelly skipped and skipped and raised the marvellous amount of £23 from family and friends who watched her skipping.

Wasn't that marvellous from someone so young?

Thank you Kelly.

Bill with his bucket and spade

Also thank you to Hans Wusterfeld and Mike Horton from Eastgate Shopping Management who allowed our Bill Crafer to go for a paddle every so often in the Roland Emmett Fantasy Clock pool in their centre.

Bill scooped the coins into his bucket to bring them back to the Hospice. The coins and Bill did get a bit wet but I think Bill enjoyed his paddle. He said it reminded him of going to the seaside.

Kelly's like a breath of fresh air to the sick

KELLY Townsend, above, is only five, but she knows all about Basildon's planned hospice.

That's why she did a sponsored skip and raised £23 for it. She said: "It's a place to make people better. And if it can't they go to Jesus in Heaven. He's looking after

Town's first hospice.

Kelly's mum, Beryl, of The Upway, Basildon, said: "When we came back from the funeral Kelly wanted to go to the grave and take some flowers.

"It was her idea to skip for money when she heard nurse Cox was collecting to open a place where people

The small child watching Bill from the side would have loved to have joined Bill in the pool I am sure.

The Eastgate shoppers were always very generous in the amount of coins they put into the pool for us. Our thanks to Eastgate Management for allowing St. Luke's to collect this money.

Our First Thanksgiving Service

During the years of active fundraising for our future hospice we wanted to thank God for supporting us, for giving us health and strength, conviction, enthusiasm and staying power.

We wanted to thank Him for all the wonderful people who came forward giving their time, their financial, practical and prayerful support.

Although the 'House on the Hill' at that time was still boarded up, waiting for the funds to start the necessary repairs, we felt it was right to hold our very first Thanksgiving Service in the future hospice grounds.

A building firm lent us some scaffolding and canvas to shield us from the inclement weather but that didn't stop us praying for sunshine.

Alan Watts, one of our very early supporters, played my keyboard and directed the choir.

Rev. David Green, our first honarary Hospice Chaplain, led the service. Michael and Jean sang a duet.

We invited all the dignitaries in our catchment area: MPs, Mayor of Thurrock, Chairman of the Council, police, ambulance and fire brigade members, our Health Authority Representatives, members of our churches, Council and Corporation and everyone whom we knew had supported us.

To mark the entrance of our 'Make-do church' I collected crazy paving and made a lovely path, with my little helper, totally unaware in those early days of Health and Safety regulations! As far as I was concerned, it was well done and safe.

Getting ready for the Thanksgiving Service before the rain !

Today, I can only shake my head and thank God, from the bottom of my heart, for watching over us to make sure that there weren't any accidents.

We did have one memorable interlude. Suddenly the heavens opened and our carefully placed tarpaulin opened up in the middle from the weight of the rain.

Apart from some of us getting wet, only my keyboard suffered. Rev. David, quick as a flash, said, 'Aah, instant baptism!' and we continued with our service.

Thankfully, it was only a short, heavenly shower, and we were able to continue celebrating and singing followed by refreshments.

Even after all these years we still remember that very first service: A barbeque, organised by Malcolm and Keith, Michael entertaining the children, Christopher playing football with some of his friends, Les and I were busy meeting all our friends, the rain and the celebrations. The laughter and the tears.

Since that first special service at the hospice we continue to hold a Thanksgiving Service every year.

999 Carol Service

As soon as we had received our official charity status we held annual carol services in various towns belonging to our catchment area.

I've selected a few of my photos to show how the 999 services - police, firefighters and ambulance members - all came together to help St. Luke's. Local shops donated gifts, helped with collections or joined us singing.

The carols were played by the Basildon Salvation Army Band and we were joined by family, friends and members of the public.

They were great occasions with everybody singing the familiar tunes and sharing the Christmas message.

999 CAROL CONCERT
IN AID OF ST. LUKES HOSPICE, BASILDON
SATURDAY 17 DECEMBER
BASILDON TOWN SQUARE
EVERYONE WELCOME
11 - 12 NOON

999 Carol Service

Hark, the mercy angels sing

999 teams join carol chorus

Lawmen combine for hospice £400,000

BIG-hearted bobbies are raking in cash for charity.

Policemen in South East Essex are getting together to raise money for the future St Luke's Hospice, Basildon.

Chief Supt. Alan Gilling told a meeting of the divisional police liaison committee: "The whole of the Basildon police division is committed. We are hoping to get Grays involved as well."

Grays division covers Stanford-le-Hope and Corringham as well as Tilbury.

Officers in the Basildon division, which includes Billericay, Wickford, Benfleet, Canvey and Hadleigh, have already started on the £400,000 appeal.

A sponsored carol concert in Basildon town centre, in which police, firemen, ambulancemen and nurses took part, raised more than £160.

And a disco at Basildon police station involving the four groups, raised more than £250. Basildon police have held darts matches and raffles too.

So far efforts throughout Essex have boosted the hospice fund to around £50,000.

Community nursing sister Trudy Cox got the project off the ground. Work will start in the spring to convert a farmhouse at Fobbing Farm near Basildon Hospital, but it will be some time before it is opened.

Mr Gilling said Basildon policemen had also been raising money for Billericay Burns Unit.

And just before Christmas, handicapped Marcus Dawes, five, whose dad is a Basildon Pc, was presented with an electric wheelchair, bought by officers from Basildon, Benfleet and Laindon.

They raised about £2,200 through taking part in marathons in London and Berlin.

It was a wonderful gesture by all the 999 emergency services to support St. Luke's in this way.

With their help our 999 Carol Services in our catchment area Wickford, Billericay, Basildon and all of Thurrock - were always a success.

Through them much needed funds were raised for the building of the hospice.

Tragedy and Miracle

On October the 22nd 1983, Les, I and Christopher accompanied Keith for a practice session to parachute for the hospice to raise funds.

We had great fun watching all the exercises, knowing we were on safe ground, while Keith had to prove himself a safe 'jumper'. Twice due to bad weather the parachute jumps had been cancelled and again this time Keith could not do the jump he was so desperate to do.

Disappointed and miserable at being denied his chance to jump, all he wanted to do was 'go home'. With his mind on other things he did not see the car that hit him.

He ended up in William Harvey Hospice, Ashford in Kent for eight weeks. At one time surgeons thought they may have to amputate his foot. But in the end they managed to save it, thank God. But it left him with a permanent limp.

But Keith being Keith, after a period of great disappointment and despair, found his natural enthusiasm and optimism again and, following his rehabilitation, used that time by supporting and helping the children at Elmbrook School, a centre for children with disabilities.

Dorothy, the head of Elmbrook School, couldn't praise Keith enough and told me that he made a real 'hit' with her pupils.

While in hospital Keith missed his graduation ceremony so the ceremony came to him.

Our photo shows Keith in his graduation gown and 'hat' surrounded by his fans, the nurses!

Although no longer able to do a parachute jump Keith continued to help us to raise funds and support us.

To this day, in his capacity as an English teacher, he is helping and encouraging me to write the story of the 'House on the Hill', St. Luke's Hospice.

At the time of writing this book Christopher has completed a tandem parachute jump for the hospice. On hearing this Keith immediately got the jumping bug again. He wants us to do a parachute jump together for St. Luke's.

I told him I'd think about it !!

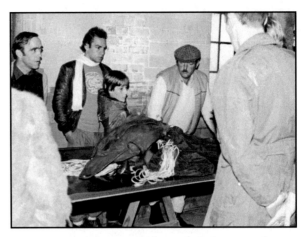

Keith, with Christopher, finding out all about parachutes

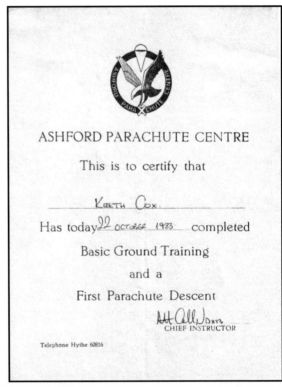

ASHFORD PARACHUTE CENTRE

This is to certify that

Keith Cox

Has today 22 October 1983 completed

Basic Ground Training

and a

First Parachute Descent

CHIEF INSTRUCTOR

Telephone Hythe 60816

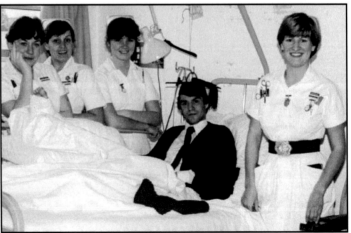

Keith being comforted by 'his' nurses

Architects - Plans - Drawings

Our Architect.

As the news of the proposed hospice spread various people came forward to help us.

One of them was a dear gentleman who offered his services in drawing up site plans for the hospice. Unfortunately, he wasn't a qualified architect with the credentials which Harry, the Chief Executive from the Corporation, pointed out to me were required. Nevertheless, we were very grateful for the offer of his help, free of charge, as it would have saved the hospice a tremendous amount of money.

I found it very hard to convey this to him, worried about finding the right words to explain. Again I asked God to please help me and give me the right words to say. The gentleman was very gracious and understood the reasons why we could not accept his wonderful and generous free offer. I felt so relieved and finally was able to sleep again at night, as all this had been a great concern for me. I am not a brave and confident person to face difficult situations and this was definitely one of them. I thanked God for finding the right words and for this lovely man.

In these early days, Dr. Jean, Ruth and I were invited by many organisations to give a talk about the proposed hospice.

One such invitation was to give a talk at the Billericay Rotary Club. Jean attended and mentioned our need for a qualified registered architect.

In the audience was Peter Strong, an architect with his premises in Billericay and he offered his services. We met with him at our 'office' in Clay Hill Road where we shared with him again the vision and need of a home for cancer patients and their families.

He asked me how I 'saw' the unit and to give him a rough drawing and believe me, it was rough, as I am no artist. Everything was so clear in my head, but unfortunately my hands and fingers aren't clever enough to put in on paper.

Peter with the town planner

Trudy with the town planner

Requirements were :

* A large lounge, a homely and comfortable place for everyone to use with facilities for tea making.

* Dining room area, individual patient's bedrooms, a separate room for our Day Care patients.

* An area set aside where In and Day Care patients could meet for a chat or to enjoy relaxation activities together.

* A hairdressing salon, a sluice and utility room, bathrooms and toilets and a treatment area where our medical equipment would be kept.

Peter got the general idea, bless him, and at one of our committee meetings presented us with his first drawings

I remember how excited I was and gave Peter a big hug. Peter is a very reserved, gentle, kind man and looked slightly worried - I am sure he had never met anyone like me before.

Architects - Plans - Drawings

Peter accepted my hug graciously and soon got used to my bubbly ways and we have remained great friends.

I will be forever grateful for his patience with me.

I have never been very good at waiting when I could see everything so clearly in my head. I certainly didn't realise how much planning and site drawings architects had to present to the council, water, gas, telephone and electricity companies.

I learned about government rules and regulations; about ground conditions, complex drainage installations; about water, gas and electricity supplies; and then there were telephone cables, foundations, rooves, windows and doors to think about.

Even in the early planning days decisions had to be made about where to put everything from electric plugs to telephone sites. I learned an awful lot!

Eventually, following many site meetings, the final plans were presented to us. How pleased we all were.

Planning the hospice with Peter over a nice cup of tea

Peter is not only a very good architect but an artist as well.

He could see the completed unit, with carpets and curtains, to give it a homely touch which we so dearly wished to make our patients and their families feel relaxed and comfortable.

At this stage we did not have enough money to proceed with the upgrading of the 'old farmhouse' - Fobbing Farm - so a decision was made to board up the 'House on the Hill'.

Fobbing Farm

It was decided it would stay like this until enough money was raised to start the actual building and reconstruction work and other preparations in readiness for the Day Care and In-Patient Unit.

So, while Peter continued to be busy getting in touch with master builders, we, in turn, continued with active fundraising.

St. Luke's boarded up

38

No Road To The Hospice

It is amazing: when you think you have hurdled all the hurdles, something else stops you in your tracks.

It seemed that everything was settled, 'The House on the Hill' secured for our future patients and then there were objections from the Council regarding the lane leading up the hill.

They felt it was too close to the road to the college and that we would have problems.

I just could not believe it. Nearly there, but not there.

Off I went to talk to the powers that were and tried my very best to persuade them that it could not be any more difficult than before with farming traffic. After all, Fobbing Farm was a farm and its latest use had been a riding school and if, horses, wagons and private cars could manage with the traffic, then surely a few ambulances, cars, patients and visitors would be able to manage.

I tried all my powers of persuasion. I was desperate. I prayed; 'Dear Lord, please, please intervene. Please let them see that it can't be any worse than all the vehicles that went up and down the lane in the past'.

Somehow the media also heard of our plight. Several articles appeared in our local newspapers.

Eventually we heard the wonderful news from the Council that access was granted.

Thank You, Lord! Thank you Whitehall! Thank you Basildon Council!

Although I could not see their reason at the time I could see it later when we lived there, when ambulances, patients, visitors and supporters all used the road.

It is difficult at times with all that traffic to-ing and fro-ing and with the heavy traffic from the hospital, drivers zooming around the roundabout with no consideration but, nevertheless, I will be ever grateful to Basildon Council for allowing us to use the lane to the House on the Hill.

Hospice is pulled up short at roundabout

BASILDON'S first hospice has run into a hitch. Its driveway cannot open out on to a roundabout.

Basildon Development Corporation has offered St Luke's hospice volunteer committee Fobbing Farm House at Nethermayne, for a peppercorn rent.

But when Essex County Council highways chiefs objected to another road entering the roundabout, which already

No route to new hospice

COUNCILLORS who visited the site of a proposed hospice have recommended rejection of the scheme until a new access is found.

Members of Essex County Council's development control committee said there were no planning objections to the hospice, but they were unhappy with the present access.

But they have asked Environment Secretary Patrick Jenkin not to grant permission for the scheme, in Nethermayne, Basildon, until this is

Victory! Hospice wins its big planning battle

A NEW hospice has won the blessing of Whitehall.

Environment Department chiefs have agreed to plans for St Luke's Hospice in Nether Mayne, Basildon.

Planners at Essex County Council had objected to the hospice driveway opening out on the busy roundabout which also serves Basildon Hospital, Basildon College and traffic feeding on to the A13.

Target

But Ministry officials say as

was unworkable and eight is now our target.

"All we need before we can officially launch the appeal is our charity registration number.

"Already local groups have done a marvellous job fundraising."

Hospice organisers promise a big official launch to raise the target £350,000 once the charity number comes through.

They have been given the hospice building by Basildon Development Corporation at low rent and with the help of

Road to the hospice

Planning Permission is granted

BASILDON DEVELOPMENT CORPORATION

NEW TOWNS ACT 1981, SECTION 7 (1)

Proposed Hospice, Fobbing Farm, Nether Mayne, Lee Chapel South, Basildon

NOTICE IS HEREBY GIVEN that the Basildon Development Corporation has submitted to the Secretary of State for the Environment under Section 7 (1) of the New Towns Act 1981, an application for approval of the conversion and extension of the former Fobbing Farmhouse, Nether Mayne, Lee Chapel South, to a Hospice for the terminally ill.

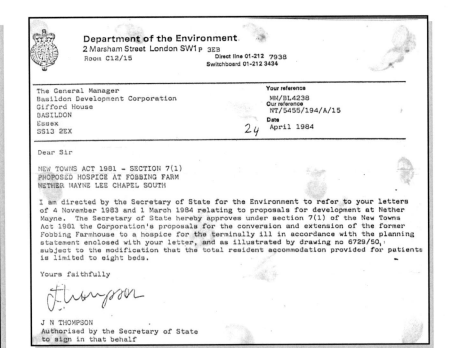

Department of the Environment.
2 Marsham Street London SW1p 3EB
Room C12/15
Direct line 01-212 7938
Switchboard 01-212 3434

	Your reference
The General Manager	MM/BL4238
Basildon Development Corporation	Our reference
Gifford House	NT/5455/194/A/15
BASILDON	Date
Essex	24 April 1984
SS13 2EX	

Dear Sir

NEW TOWNS ACT 1981 - SECTION 7(1)
PROPOSED HOSPICE AT FOBBING FARM
NETHER MAYNE LEE CHAPEL SOUTH

I am directed by the Secretary of State for the Environment to refer to your letters of 4 November 1983 and 1 March 1984 relating to proposals for development at Nether Mayne. The Secretary of State hereby approves under section 7(1) of the New Towns Act 1981 the Corporation's proposals for the conversion and extension of the former Fobbing Farmhouse to a hospice for the terminally ill in accordance with the planning statement enclosed with your letter, and as illustrated by drawing no 6729/50, subject to the modification that the total resident accommodation provided for patients is limited to eight beds.

Yours faithfully

J N THOMPSON
Authorised by the Secretary of State
to sign in that behalf

Meanwhile, applications had been submitted to the Secretary of State for approval to convert the farmhouse into a hospice.

In April 1984 we heard the good news that we had received planning permission from the Department of the Environment for Fobbing Farm to be converted into a hospice for the terminally ill.

On this page is the planning application notice, details from our architect and a letter from the Department of the Environment.

JOHN STRONG & PARTNERS

Chartered Architects 88a High Street Billericay Essex CM12 9BT

Dear Trudy,

Telephone 027 74 3101/2

Attached is some good news regarding 27 April 1984. the planning approval for Fobbing Farm. I am sending a similar copy to Jean Maxwell in the same post.

With Compliments

Trust your course is going well. Kind regards to Les.

Yours sincerely, Peter Strong.

Happy smiles all round as the planning application is approved

A page from my album at the time....

St. Luke's Hospice

Founders: Mr. & Mrs. C.H. Cox
214 Clay Hill Road, Basildon, Essex. SS16 4AA Tel: Basildon (0268) 24973

... but the greatest of these is love ...
1 Corinthians 13 V.13

ST. LUKE'S HOSPICE,
WE CARE.

Dear Friends

A year has passed since my last letter to you. Please forgive the absence of the summer letter, but I so wanted to commence it with the words:

"The work on the Hospice has started!"

But the Lord's timing and our timing doesn't always coincide. I had to learn the very hard lesson of waiting - being patient. Those of you who know me personally know just how hard that is for me.

But at the times when I felt lowest and most despondent the prayers you sent to the Lord on my behalf helped and supported me. I would like to thank all of you who so faithfully continued to pray for St. Luke's Hospice and for those who are involved in raising the money to commence the building works. Our prays have been answered! Permission has been given to commence with the drainage work which was our biggest problem. So in January the Hospice will no longer stand unattended with its windows boarded up. The builders are moving in and work will commence then.

Please continue to support us in your various ways. In prayers for us who are directly involved in establishing St. Luke's Hospice. P   need our help: the sick, lonely and bereaved. They need our prayers in

The scaffolding goes up and the builder's machines arrive.....

BUILDING FUND FOR PROPOSED
ST. LUKE'S HOSPICE
DEVELOPMENT ON THIS SITE
DONATIONS TO
SISTER TRUDY COX
C/o BASILDON POLICE STATION
BASILDON 26011

Repairing and Refurbishing the 'House on the Hill' Fobbing Farm - Phase 1

Wonderful news - enough money has been raised to commence the refurbishing of the farmhouse and the preparation work for the new extension. Finally the day came when the builders removed the boards and wrapped scaffolding all around the farmhouse. They arrived with their lorries, tractors, tools, cement, bricks and started digging.

It was a marvellous moment for which we had all waited so long. By now six years had passed since I had first made public the vision of a hospice in our area and now the moment had arrived. Thank you, God.

Thank you everyone who helped to raise the necessary funds to make this possible

We were so excited, especially my children and my family,

They say, every picture tells a story and here is our story in photographs...

The builders first task was to fix a major crack in an outside wall.

The wall had to come down and be re-built.

Next problem was the main drainage.... there wasn't any !

Drains, Drainage, Pipes & 'Cesspools'

Once work started on the Fobbing Farm site, I quickly had to learn many new building words and technical details -- main drainage and sewage, utility services, (gas, electric and water) and cesspools. I'd never heard of cesspools before but I soon found out about it all and Fobbing Farm had one !

It had to go !

Please don't drop me ....!

Where's Christopher gone???!!

These really were wonderful and exciting times.

After lots of hard work by many people, fundraising, giving freely of their time and many prayers we were finally building our hospice - St Luke's.

Of course, there were still going to be problems ahead, setbacks and tears, but we had finally begun the journey to start the building work and we were so happy.

As you can see, we were determined to enjoy some laughs along the way.

Mud, mud, glorious mud.

No, it's not Bill & Ben, the Flowerpot Men - it's Michael and Keith.

Michael, Keith and Malcolm having fun

Fobbing Farm - vandals - boarded up - repairs - prayers

Having received our charity number and overcome the problems of access 'to the House on the Hill', Fobbing Farm was now boarded up for the time being.

I continued working as a District Nursing Sister and Les as Manager at Billericay Service Station but, in our spare time, worked hard to raise the necessary funds for the essential repairs to the old farmhouse to make it habitable. Money was needed to repair: windows, doors, floors and boiler, in preparation for the extension that will eventually be a home for our patients during their time of need.

Once a month I organised a support group for cancer patients and their families and bereavement support.

At weekends we started holding volunteer training courses in order to have a group of trained volunteers ready when our patient care started in earnest.

Jean, Ruth and I continued giving talks to various groups - Rotary, Round Table and Lions, Inner Wheel, businesses, churches and schools, in fact, anyone who would invite us to share with them the vision of a hospice in our catchment area. From Thurrock, right down to the Thames at Purfleet, this catchment area included South Ockendon, Grays, Stanford le Hope, Corringham, Fobbing, Billericay, Wickford and Basildon with a population of approximately 300,000.

While the house was boarded up the vandals had a great time. On numerous occasions the house was broken into. The intruders set about destroying whatever they fancied. I was heartbroken and just could not understand that people could be that wicked to do such a thing.

The police, Les and I met frequently, looking at the damage and doing emergency repair work.

Damage -- and -- repair

Gib mir die Gelassenheit, Dinge hinzunehmen, die ich nicht ändern kann. Gib mir den Mut, Dinge zu ändern, die ich ändern kann und gib mir die Weisheit, das eine vom andern zu unterscheiden!

Give me the calmness to accept the things I cannot alter.

Give me the courage to alter things which I can alter.

Give me the wisdom to distinguish one from the other.

German prayer with the English translation above.

A prayer that helped me a lot at this time was a German one I had on a card in my pocket. It is printed here with the English translation.

As a committee we decided then that we, as a family, should live on the premises once the repairs were completed so that the house and grounds would not be so isolated.

New Appointment - Les, The Administrator

Our dining room in our Clay Hill Road house continued to be his official office for the time being. Les took a big step in faith by leaving a secure position and committing himself to full time work at the charity that was so dear to his heart, St. Luke's Hospice.

The following are excerpts from the Trustees Report and various good wishes and prayers of encouragement he received.

TRUSTEES REPORT

Present total amount raised for St. Luke's Hospice £134,000.00

From the outset, as you know, it has always been the intention that Mr. Les Cox would be Administrator at the Hospice. As work on the Hospice is due to commence, and it has become increasingly apparent that we need someone to co-ordinate activities on a full-time basis, and be on the spot to oversee the building work day by day it was decided that 'now' was the time to ask Les to take up this appointment.

You will know only too well the great burden of work that is placed on Trudy, who has a full-time job and a home to run, and others with similar commitments. All in all the project has reached the stage when it is necessary to take this major major step.

It was a big decision for Les to take - leaving the job he has hedd for 27 years and stepping out into the unknown as it were, and we are more than confident that he will meet the challenge of this demanding job.

To dear Les,
May our Lord bless you as you take another step in faith.

Loving thoughts are with you,

may God bless you today

With our love + prayers,
Trudy, Christopher, Gerry,
Judy, Edna, Ruth Jean,
Pat and Jenny.

Dear Trudy & Les

Knowing folks
as nice as you
is a blessing and a pleasure
And this special card will tell you,
in at least a little measure,
That We are glad and thankful, too,
to know someone as nice as you.

With all our love
and thanks for more
than you realize.
Our fondest.
Love Eileen & Sid
x x x

45

More best wishes for new Administrator Les

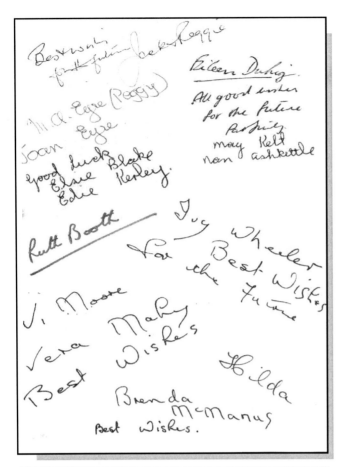

Thank you Les, for all
your help,

Trudy

Cox Family Move to Fobbing Farm

The House on the Hilll.....Boards are removed......We move in .....

The day arrived to leave our house in Clay Hill Road and move into that precious 'House on the Hill' - Fobbing Farm, Les, Christopher and I, with our little Battersea Dog's Home puppy, 'Rocky'.

It turned out to be a very memorable day all around for, right in the middle of driving

back and forth from Clay Hill Road to Fobbing Farm taking our belongings to our new home, our very first grand-daughter was born; Danielle, on 11th September 1986. What wonderful news, our first 'Hospice Baby'.

We were excited and very busy that day. Travelling to the hospice, then back to Clay Hill Road, then to the hospital and in the evening a toast - new baby - new temporary home.

Trudy and Les curtain making for the 'new' home

We soon gave Fobbing Farm the 'homely touch'.

We became tenants - caretakers - jumble and bric a brac receivers - as well as welcoming the many visitors who saw the sign 'proposed hospice' outside and came to find out what it was all about .

We continued in our 'new' home with monthly cancer and bereavement support, meetings, volunteer training courses continued, cramped in the downstairs sitting room (which now became the Finance Office).

Candlelit Advent Evening celebrations at Fobbing Farm

I am sure our friends still remember candlelit Advent evenings in our 'new' home during the Christmas periods.

Our talented singers entertaining us: with Vernon on my keyboard, Alan and his singers and everyone celebrating the coming of Christmas.

These are fond memories of the early days.

Jumble sales on the proposed Hospice site - Fobbing Farm

From our house in Clay Hill Road we brought our little 'garden house' with us, which was converted into a tea room. All around us jumble and bric-a-brac needed sorting, labelling, cleaning and selling.

Family and friends and our band of fundraisers were busy keeping the whole scene in order as our visitors enjoyed their afternoon tea whilst browsing and buying.

Cox Family move to Fobbing Farm

In 1986 Les left his job as manager of Billericay Service Station to become the full time Hospice Administrator.

I continued working as a District Nurse for a further year before I retired from the NHS. Jean, Ruth and I carried on giving talks, encouraging our community to support the Hospice.

More volunteers and helpers came forward. The support we were getting was truly amazing. We were all very grateful to everyone who came to help us.

Les and Christopher sort out the office

Les, during this time, continued to be very busy as Administrator. The telephone rang continuously and much post had to be dealt with to answer all the enquiries, financial issues and, we had attend the numerous meetings with our architect and engineers.

Les being Les, everything had to be in tip-top order.

He was definitely the best person to keep us all on our toes. We often teased him about being so meticulous and particular, photocopying everything and his filing system was absolutely superb.

I often had to eat humble pie, confessing that I had lost something. Time and again he helped me by producing an important document I had mislaid.

I will always be grateful to Les for being so careful and correct. I am just not an office person and have always found it hard doing all the paperwork that was expected of me. Thank you, Les, for your help (for a damsel in distress).

'Guard-dogs' Rocky and Lady

I should mention we had two other important members of the Cox family moving in with us at Fobbing Farm; our two 'guard dogs' - Rocky and Lady.

Rocky, (Cox family - 'guard dog' - I don't think so - too soft like the rest of the Cox Family), was Christopher's pet. Soon he was joined by Lady. Both of the dogs came from Battersea Dog's Home.

Altogether we lived in the upstairs flat in Fobbing Farm for six years until the Autumn of 1992.

It meant living at the hospice for the first two years St. Luke's was open. But this was a conscious decision on my part.

I wanted to make sure before I left that the hospice was running as I felt it should be as a 'Hospice Family Home' and all the staff and volunteers were settled in.

I think it was the right decision to take and that the ethos set in motion then is still carried out today.

Our second grand-daughter, Nicola, was born in 1988 while we were still at Fobbing Farm

Picnic in the Grounds

Fobbing Farm now became our new home for the next six years.

It took a little while for us to settle in, and cram into the flat upstairs. but to make us feel at home family and friends visited.

My photograph on this page shows a picnic in the 'Hospice Garden' with members of Fryerns Baptist Church and my family.

We held many jumble sales, coffee mornings and afternoon teas in the area in front of the farmhouse to raise money for the new planned extension.

Apart from one or two unpleasant incidents where we had unwelcome visitors wanting to damage the farm

house it was the right decision to live on the premises as caretakers.

At this time we also put up our first thermometer sign up for passing traffic to indicate the money raised so far.

Betty Phillips and Lesley.

One day, while I was updating the sign, a lady stopped me and told me about her daughter, Lesley.

Lesley had been admitted into the Royal Marsden Hospital in London suffering from an advanced cancer and, sadly, died there.

While in the Royal Marsden, Lesley had written poems about hospital life - staff, food and others.

Betty and Mick, her husband, decided to have the poems published and the royalties were to be shared between St. Luke's Hospice and Cancer Research.

This was obviously a very sad and difficult time for Lesley's family but they continue to support the hospice.

Betty eventually became the manager in one of our charity shops in South Ockendon and she still is at the time of printing.

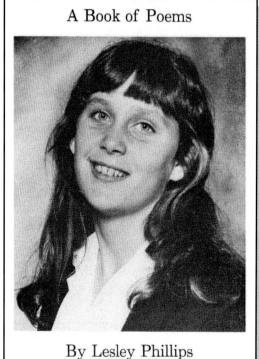

A Book of Poems

By Lesley Phillips

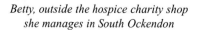

Betty, outside the hospice charity shop she manages in South Ockendon

The Times I Nearly Gave Up

The next few years were very busy. Both Les and I continued our daily jobs - he, as Hospice Administrator and I as a District Nurse.

When not on duty as a District Nurse I continued with fundraising, the training of volunteers, monthly bereavement and cancer support meetings, with meetings with the Hospice Management team to plan and discuss future developments.

Those years were hard work but we had a lot of fun especially with our market stalls, jumble sales, and many other hospice fundraising events.

Mingled among these memories were also difficult times when I did feel like giving up. I was very tearful and sometimes felt I just couldn't go on.

Here's why and here are my responses:

1) I was accused of using donated public funds to buy food, clothes and personal items for myself and my family and not using it for the hospice.

Answer... The public couldn't see anything happening. They didn't know that we attended many meetings with architects, engineers and builders. They didn't and couldn't see the work here in the old farmhouse in the cellar where boilers were installed in readiness for heating the future extension.

Most of the preparation work was being carried out underground and not visible. Because of this they thought their donations were not being used to build a hospice.

2) On another occasion I was accused of being a hypocrite by a member of my church. This person said, "If your God wants this hospice to happen then your God should provide. There shouldn't be a need for fundraising., Why ask us for money".

Answer... My God did and does provide to this day. He provided people to help and support us. He gave us hearts to be compassionate and to share his love. I call it "love in action". He gave us the opportunity to learn skills and gain knowledge, and to think of ever new fundraising ideas. He gave us hands and feet to work for Him and those who needed our help. He gave us strength to continue even during difficult times.

3) An added problem was my often poor general health. Early in my childhood I spent many months in hospital which has left me with a chronic chest complaint and vulnerable for the rest of my life.

I was often very tired. I found it difficult to cope with all the added demands on my time and the responsibilities I was having to face.

But these moments passed. I had and have excellent medical consultants who make sure that I stay well.

4) I was always worried about being so busy as a District Nurse and trying to establish the hospice that I was neglecting my own family. It was always hard leaving them, as I had to, because the nature of my work demanded unsocial hours. Time and again they reassured me not to worry about them. They all helped and encouraged me.

So here I am, after all these years, thankful for my loving and understanding family and to God who gave me strength and, I know, watches over me. The prayer below was in my office and was a constant source of encouragement

Morning Prayer
Lord help me
to remember
that nothing is going
to happen to me
today
that you and I together
can't handle

Royal Marsden Hospital

Having been accepted to attend the Royal Marsden course in palliative care together my friend, Sue, and I travelled daily to London, battling our way through busy rush hour traffic. Arriving at the Royal Marsden Hospital we joined our colleagues to attend the course "Care of the dying Patient and his family".

In those early days this was the only specified course in palliative care dealing with patients suffering from cancer.

The course was very intensive but it was good to learn that there are so many different approaches to help those who are suffering pain and dealing with very difficult to manage symptoms as well as attending to their emotional, social and spritual needs. Sue and I completed our course and returned to our families tired but full of enthusiasm in the hope of making life a little easier for our patients and their families.

But it didn't work out like that. I became more and more frustrated and sometimes even angry. I realised that the course I had just attended at the Marsden teaching us the excellent management that could be attained in the care of the cancer patients was not yet in place in our area.

Many of my patients continued to suffer unnecessarily. We couldn't take the disease away but surely we could make life more bearable for them?

The GPs I worked with were a mixture of really good, caring doctors, up-to-date in the new developments in pain and symptom control and patient management. Men and women who really cared and put themselves out for our patients and those who had not attended specific courses in palliative care and consequently were not totally aware of all the new developments, and certainly didn't want to hear it from a mere 'District Nurse'.

I could well understand why Dame Cecily Saunders, a nurse and founder of the modern Hospice movement decided the only way she could help her patients more was by training and becoming a doctor herself.

Then she could prescribe the appropriate medication herself.

But I wasn't Dame Cecily. I was just me, and what's more, I loved nursing. I wanted to care for my patients as a nurse.

My colleagues with me at the Royal Marsden

I felt I had wasted my time and energy attending the Royal Marsden course. Although if I hadn't, I would have just soldiered on not knowing that more could be done. That pain and symptoms could be controlled better, emotional pain and distress could be eased, spiritual concerns addressed and financial and social problems attended to.

First I resigned myself but then I couldn't stand it any longer. I had been hoping for a long time that someone would come along and change things, but that someone never happened.

Macmillan Service in the Thurrock, Basildon area and District Nurses support

Whilst waiting for the moment when building work would commence I spent a day in London.

It had surprised and saddened me that there wasn't a Macmillan Service in our area of Thurrock, Basildon, Billericay and Wickford.

I had made an appointment with their head office in London to ask for the possibility of developing this Service in our catchment area.

I explained to them that we were in the process of establishing a hospice in Thurrock and Basildon, serving a population of approximately 300,000. Included in our catchment area are: Thurrock, with Corringham, Fobbing, Stanford le Hope, Grays & Tilbury as well as Basildon, Billericay and wickford. At this time there weren't any funds to have our own St. Luke's Macmillan nurse.

Although they were very sympathetic they felt our charity status at that time wasn't enough to convince them that we would be able to pick up the financial commitment after 3 years.

To explain - MacMillan Service provide for the first three years salary for their nurses but then they need a guarantee that the Service will continue after the initial help from them. Well, we couldn't give them this guarantee, as all the monies raised needed to go to establish our hospice.

After discussions I invited members of the District Nurses Management and Nurse Manager from Basildon Hospital and Macmillan representatives to a joint meeting in the old farmhouse, - Fobbing Farm - our new home, (downstairs in the lounge which now serves as our finance office).

Macmillan Service agreed to fund a Macmillan Nurse in our area for three years and the Health Authority committed themselves to picking up the salary bill after that.

How pleased and relieved I felt. Now there would also be a Macmillan Service in our area and we at the hospice would work closely with them. Basildon Hospital would provide accommodation.

A few years later in 1996 we were eventually able to have our own St. Luke's Hospice Macmillan Nurse. She continued to be based at the hospital and work together with her colleagues there as a liaison between hospital and hospice and the Macmillan Service.

Terminal Care panel team meeting at St. Luke's. Included are representatives from Basildon and South Hospital, Mcmillan and District Nurse colleagues and hospice staff.
These meetings continue to be held at St. Luke's Hospice

My nursing colleagues study the plans for the hospice

I would like at this time to place on record my thanks to all my District Nursing colleagues who supported me wholeheartedly in my quest to establish a home for cancer patients in our area.

Their support meant a lot to me.

Thank you all so much.

Trudy leaves the NHS as District Nurse

I had now worked as a District Nursing Sister for nearly 26 years, but the time was right for me to retire from the NHS to commence my work as Matron for St. Luke's Hospice. Although I really looked forward to this moment, it also felt very disconcerting and scary.

Would I manage the responsibility that was now mine? Did God give me more than I could handle.

My sister, Irmgard, knowing how I felt, sent me this card She told me not to become despondent.

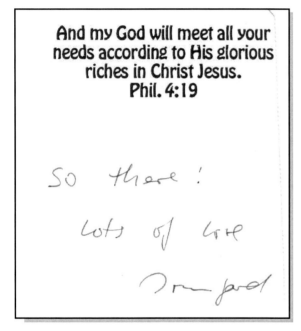

And my God will meet all your needs according to His glorious riches in Christ Jesus.
Phil. 4:19

So there!

Lots of Love

Irmgard

My leaving presentation from my colleagues at the NHS

It felt good to know and have the reassurance that God is in control and my prayers during these months were asking him for health and strength, and most of all, for confidence for the task ahead.

Les, as always, encouraged and reassured me.

The next year continued to be a very busy one. There were the monthly Cancer and Bereavement Support meetings as well as continuing giving talks about the vision of a Home for cancer patients and their families.

VAT Shock

Would you believe it.

We had sorted out the problem with the vandals and then another one appears.

The taxman is not kind to us at all. We just wanted to help our patients by providing a home for them, where they could find love and comfort, where we would help them with some distressing symptoms so the remainder of their life would be free of pain and the patient and their families would be looked after by caring staff and volunteers.

We work hard in raising the necessary funds. We have children and pensioners and the rest of us all trying to think up new fundraising ideas. Then the tax man comes along and wants his pound of flesh.

The newspaper articles tell the story.

The VAT problem was eventually solved by losing some hospice space. The ruling was - the new extension could not be attached to the old farm house. So, we had to make the new building stand on its own. New buildings for the hospice would be tax free, but additions would incur VAT. Crazy, maybe, but that's the law.

The press cuttings say it all. One appeared in the 'Evening Echo' 18th June 1984. The other is from the front page of the 'Standard Recorder' 22nd June 1984.

The Conservative Central Governmment at that time had added V.A.T. to building work - without any exemption for charities - which effectively raised the cost of constructing the hospice by a further £55,000. Mr Peaty's appeal to the local Tory MPs, Harvey Proctor and David Amess, predictably produced no results as they followed party lines.

But it did all end in smiles for Gerry and Trudy. They solved the VAT problem by agreeing not to attach the new building directly to the Fobbing Farmhouse, instead they linked the two buildings with a glass verandah.

Problem solved.

Evening Echo 18.6.84

VAT shock puts up cost of hospice

THE taxman has added a shock £55,000 to the cost of building a town's new hospice.

Now angry Basildon hospice organisers are asking their MPs for help to fight VAT on building work.

They have had new figures from their architects this we

£55,000 VAT to building St Luke's.

Treasurer Mr Gerald Peaty said: "Just as we got our charity number ready to steam ahead with appeal work, we got our latest cost revision.

"It will now cost £400,000 on present prices. When we started planning . . . . ago it was £200,000."

VATastic

THE cost of building a home for the incurably ill in Basildon has doubled — from £200,000 to £400,000 — in less than a year.

Shocked organisers of the St Luke's Hospice fund have been stunned with the latest news — that an extra £55,000 will be needed to cover VAT charges imposed at the last budget. The rest is in increased building costs since the first estimates were made.

Fund treasurer Gerald Peaty is now organising a meeting with local Tory MPs David Amess and Harvey Proctor in the hope of getting the VAT waived.

Plea over hospice's . . . ax shock

. . . RITY to help the dying faces a £158,000

£¼ million needs to be raised to open . . . Luke's Hospice in Basildon. A large . . . cost is VAT on the building im- . . . the town's MP David Amess told the Commons.

He urged the Government to lift the VAT burden, or make the . . . .

All smiles as the VAT problem is solved

Foundation Stone Ceremony

Finally the exciting day arrived when we would be celebrating the Foundation Stone Ceremony.

Preparations for this special day had been in place for some time.

Invitations had been sent out to our VIP guests: our Basildon MP David Amess, the Chairman of Basildon Council Mr Frank Tomlin, Chief Executive of the Commission for New Town, Mr Harry Bacon, Father Brian, representing our Catholic Community, my hospital physician, Dr. Lee, representatives of the Lions, Rotary, Round Table, Inner Wheel, and many other organisations.

Thanks to the generosity of Basildon Health Authority we had the use of two of their marquees. A team from the old South Ockendon Hospital came and put them up for us.

Everyone involved were rewarded for all their hard work with a full English breakfast served by Kathy, who later became the St. Luke's Cook/Housekeeper.

Rob, from Basildon Council
proudly raises the flag

The Foundation Stone ceremony was led by our then Hospice Chaplain Rev. Derek Tuck, from Socketts Heath Baptist church.

Vernon, from Stanford le Hope Methodist church, played the keyboard organ for us during the ceremony.

Our local MP, David Amess, laid our Foundation Stone, watched by members of his family and the hospice family and guests.

It was a very emotional moment for all of us.

After years of hard work fundraising to start our local hospice, we did feel we were finally achieving our goal - a hospice in our area.

Foundation Stone Ceremony

Following the Foundation Stone ceremony we held a Thanksgiving Celebration Service in the marquee, led by the Rev. Derek Tuck.

Michael and Jean Rawlinson sang 'Bless This House O Lord we pray' to us as a song of dedication.

Cllr. Frank Tomlin, Chairman Basildon Council

Cllr .David Harrison, Basildon Council

Mrs Joan Martin, OBE, Basildon and Thurrock Health Authority

Dr Ying Lee, my Basildon Hospital Consultant

Alan Gilling, Chief of Police

Father Brian, RC priest

Harry Bacon, Chief Executive, Basildon Corporation

David Amess, MP for Basildon

The Rev. Derek Tuck

Jean & Michael Rawlinson

Basildon Salvation Army Band

My photographs opposite show some of the speakers and representatives of our community bringing greetings from their various organistions.

The Salvation Army Band from Basildon played for us as we shared light refreshments together prepared by Kathy and some of our volunteers.

Foundation Stone Ceremony

At the end of the day, the clearing up began.

There was a lot to do but our hospice volunteers soon got to work: carrying and stacking, lifting and storing, until the hospice site was ready for the next stage of building to begin.

Later we enjoyed a bar-be-cue manned by my sons Michael and Keith together with our 'adopted' son No 4, Malcolm

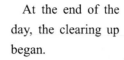
Roy Smith-photographer

During the day a nursery nurse was on hand looking after our little people. Roy Smith, radio presenter and photographer was there, as always, taking photographs.

What a Memorable Day !!

A Moment To Reflect

A few days later Les and I went back to have our photographs taken by the Foundation Stone. It had really been a momentous day in the life of St. Luke's. It was a day, too, to thank God for all his help in bringing us to this day. We also received the letter below from Julia Amess which pleased us greatly.

HOUSE OF COMMONS
LONDON SW1A 0AA

DAVID AMESS MP
Member of Parliament for Basildon

18th July, 1988

Dear Trudy + Les,

Just a very quick note to thank you (and those who were involved) for choosing David to lay the foundation stone for St. Lukes. I just can't tell you how honoured we both were when you asked him and how proud I was to attend the ceremony and watch him with the trowel!!

The day was lovely and the service was perfect – I think that the children behaved well bearing in mind that they are at their worst at that time of day!

Thank you for including me in your special day and I know that without two people such as yourselves, none of it would have been possible. Well done!

Much Love to you all,

Julia
xx

This was the completion of Phase One

More Fundraising

As you are reading this book you will see that throughout all these pages you will find many different fundraising events.

These obviously had to go on throughout the development so that we could complete the building project. And then we needed to continue fundraising to cover the running costs.

One of our biggest fundraising events were our Fun Days in Basildon Town Centre. We held them yearly for five years.

We also held Fun Days in Corringham Town Centre, Grays, Tilbury and other local areas .

Our Basildon Fun Days always ended with a march up to the House on the Hill - St. Luke's.

The police closed the roads, police horses led the way, followed by the marching bands and everyone who had taken part.

Fun Days

In The
Town Centres

Fun Days in Our Town Centres

Preparing for our Fun-day in Basildon Town Centre was hard work and demanded a big commitment from everyone but they were great fun.

The Police premises at Basildon Town Centre, Tilbury, Grays and the church hall Corringham became our 'official planning rooms', where our preparation meetings for our Fundraising Fun Days were held.

Together with our friendly Police, Fire and Ambulance Service and volunteers, from St. Luke's, and Malcolm, from the Basildon Corporation Planning Department, plans were discussed for the big celebrations.

The more ideas and suggestions were flying around, the more excited we all became. In the meantime, most of the stores in the Town Centres advertised the events by placing posters and handing out leaflets. Our local radio did us proud by announcing our events.

Our first big Fun Day was celebrated in Basildon Town Centre. In fact we almost took over the town square, from the escalator to the mother and child sculpture. Community spirit was running high!!

The police, firemen and ambulance services, as well as churches, schools, scouts and guides, brownies, local businessmen joined in collecting and helping with fundraising.

Some of our friends dressed up as clowns, as Alice and the Mad Hatter and many other characters.

The Centre stage, was the trailer from Peter's Barleylands farm where Roy, from Basildon Radio, stood making the announcements and introducing everyone.

David, our MP, and our Chairman from Basildon Council, joined us on stage, giving us all a warm welcome and encouragement in our efforts to raise our much needed funds to build the Hospice.

My nieces from Germany, Kirstin and Heinke, joined by their friends Hazel and Kathy on their guitars, with their friend on her accordian entertained everyone.

They were followed by Ghyllgrove School Children's Choir singing their little hearts out conducted by Jean, their music teacher.

Our Fun Day In Basildon Town Centre

A big attraction at our Fun Days was our sale of 'symbolic' bricks. We laid out a big pile of bricks and our son Keith was soon selling bricks like hot cakes. I think he quite enjoyed being an auctioneer for a day.

He even sold one to our local MP at that time, David Amess.

All the buyers received a paper brick designed by children from Chalvedon school as a formal receipt.

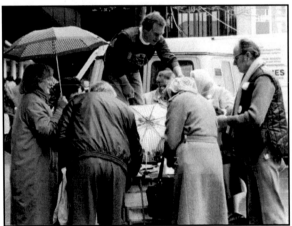

DE: Scouts and cubs stand by stacks of bricks for sale.

St Luke's big day

ST LUKE'S Hospice will stage a day of dedication on Saturday, as part of their building appeal.

The special day has been arranged to mark the handover of Fobbing Farm, in Nethermayne, and the official commencement of the building programme to convert the farmhouse into a hospice for the terminally ill.

Events planned include majorettes, children's choirs, processions of horses, and bands. They take place in Basildon Town Square from 2pm.

Members of the public will be invited to 'buy a brick'. All the bricks will be taken to the

Fun day was a block buster

he bands played rack Your Troubles and they ched with their heads n. Some danced to keep m.

olin Rigby, 20, of berley Road, Benfleet, bled along on crutches de his band, Hadleigh rching Militaire.

'arade marshall John en, of Boytons, Basildon, l: "He sprained his le, but he was determined to be left out. I was proud the young people's onse."

rs Trudy Cox, of Clay

matron of the hospice, said: "It was fantastic.

"When I saw that procession of young people I nearly cried."

At the open-air dedication on the hospice site, near Basildon Sports Centre, the weather gave the Rev David Greaves the joke of the day.

The wind blew the tarpaulin roof aside and water collected on it cascaded inside, causing people to move hastily.

Mr Greaves went to the microphone and asked: "Is there anyone who hasn't

BRIC-A-BRAC: Keith Cox finds a ready custo

Clowns, Clowns, Clowns ...

Another sell-out attraction at all our 'Fun Days' were those wonderful people who put on the greasepaint, the funny hats and shoes and became our clowns for a day.

Can you recognise any of the faces behind the clowns smiles?

Our clowns were not only seen in Basildon. They were with us at all our Fun Days, in Tilbury, Stanford le Hope, Corringham and Grays

Our wonderful collecting clowns - and the young children helped, too. My thanks to them all.

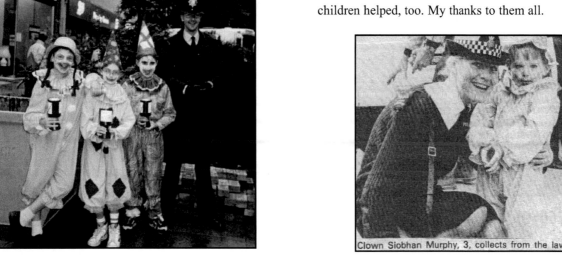

Clown Siobhan Murphy, 3, collects from the law

More clowns - the young ones,
and the not so young
were always ready to help

Fun Days Continued ...

*The local bands and majorettes were great supporters of our Fun Days in Basildon Town Centre
but don't be deceived by the sunny photos I've selected here - our Fun Days had its fair share
of rainy days but the bands and majorettes still turned up to perform their displays for us.*

Bonanza day for hospice

FUN-day in aid of St ke's Hospice, Basildon, ned into a bonanza.

Shoppers in the Town uare dug deep into their ckets, handing over £5 and 0 notes to nudge nearer to e day's £1,000 target.

In the event, much more as raised, as hoolchildren, youth oups, bands, shops and the nergency services linked in mammoth effort.

Trudy Cox said she was overwhelmed by the support and overjoyed at the amount raised for the hospice, at Fobbing Farm, Nethermayne.

The day finished with a mile-long procession winding up the hill from the town to the hospice.

Mrs Cox said: "I must admit as I walked up I turned and looked back at the procession and had a lump in my throat. It was absolutely wonderful."

Trudy Cox, MP David Amess, Town Cryer Bill Morris and Coun David Harrison accept cheque from Charrington for £433

Fun Days Continued ...

I've included these photographs to give you an idea of how St. Luke's, with the help of the 999 services, really did take over our local town centres on our Fun Days.

I cannot thank the local authorities enough for allowing us to do this.

The ambulance teams and the firefighters took the opportunity to teach everyone how they deal with emergencies, as well as helping us to fundraise.

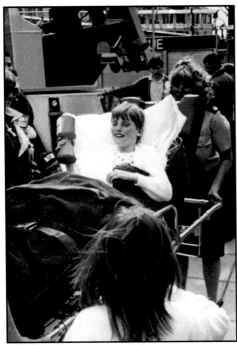

Firefighters at the top of their high ladders always brought a buzz of excitement, especially when one of our volunteers was at the top as well !

Ambulance crews joined in, teaching us first aid as well as raising funds, and at the same time keeping a watchful eye out for any real first aid needs.

Children were allowed to inspect the fire engines, ambulances and police vans with our friends from the 999 services explaining how they deal with emergenciese.

Fun Days Continued ...

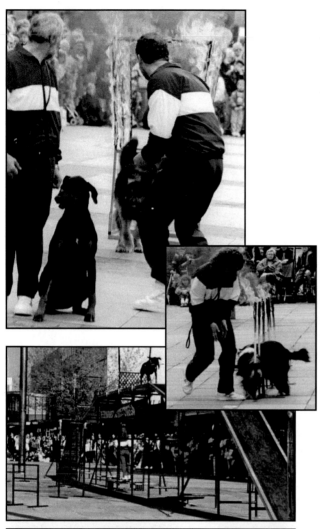

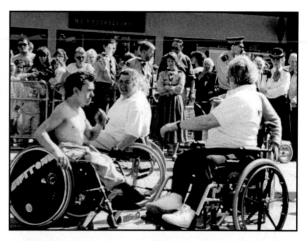

As you can see we tried to cater for all tastes and interests.

From dogs jumping through flaming hoops and running across ramps, to a game of basketball from wheelchair bound sportsmen.

We had Herr Ernst and his Oom Pah band to provide the music. M&S Management had opened up their doors and cafeteria for refreshments and allowed us to use their rest-room facilities.

Tea and cakes were organised by Marks & Spencer staff members Sandra and Maureen and their colleagues.

Fun Day Town Criers

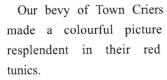

Herr Ernst from the Oom Pah band even took up the challenge to teach Bill Crafer and the Town Crier how to dance a German waltz !!

Our bevy of Town Criers made a colourful picture resplendent in their red tunics.

There are some well known local faces hidden behind the costumes. Can you identify them ?

The days were always hard work but full of fun as well as raising thousands of pounds to help to establish our hospice.

68

Fun Days Continued ...

Our volunteer face painters were soon overrun by children wanting their faces painted and our stallholders were kept busy selling their goods.

Our celebrations began with the music of the Sutherland Pipes and Drums.

The hospice Information Desk always attracted many enquiries from people wanting to know more about our hopes for establishing a hospice.

We even had royalty - a Pearly King and Queen joined us, too !

Ken Revell, took on the role of 'Burlington Bertie', although I am not sure how the kiddies bicycle fitted in.

But it was all in keeping with our idea of a Fun Day for everyone.

At the end of the celebration, a procession was formed in front of Basildon Police Station ready for the march out of the town centre and up the hill to the site of the new hospice.

It was led by police horses, police motorbikes, fire engines, ambulances, Sutherland Pipes and Drums, many local marching bands and majorettes, boys' and girls' brigades, cubs and scout groups, children from various schools and Sunday schools, accompanied by parents, teachers and friends.

March To The Hospice Site

The march from the town centre to the House on the Hill seemed like a great exodus with people on foot, crutches or in wheelchairs, following the procession.

The roads were cordoned off, made safe and supervised by our friendly police force with members of their special police.

Arriving At The Hospice Site

Who was it who said people these days don't care and only look out for themselves? Come and see us, we can prove you wrong !!!

How fortunate we were, or are, living among such a caring, helpful and enthusiastic community.

When arriving at the House on the Hill, I turned around and tears filled my eyes when looking back at the long procession down at the Town Centre up Nethermayne and reaching the hospice site.

We were greeted by the welcoming sound of a marching band, with an official welcome, and the delicious aroma of a barbecue and refreshments prepared by our family, friends and volunteers. What a wonderful day was had by all.

Following that first Fundraising Day in Basildon Town Centre we were able to repeat these celebrations four more times. As well as Fun Days in Basildon remember we also held them in Corringham, tilbury and Grays.

Each time we were able to make it bigger and better, with more and more schools, marching bands, displays and entertainment taking part.

On our later Town Centre Fun Day marches our first Day Care patients were able to join in the welkcome to us. It was wonderful to see their smiling faces. It made all the hard fundraising worth it and, after all, that was what it was all about.

Our thanks to everyone involved for their help, commitment and enthusiasm to make it all possible.

So many people from so many different backgrounds, all supporting us by giving their time, talents, money and making everyone aware that a new home for cancer patients and their families was about to become a reality.

Thank you again so much everyone.

A well-earned barbecue and refreshments for the Fun Day helpers

Our Fun Day Thanksgiving Services

Rival politicians told to join hands and sing 'Bind Us Together Lord'

A PREACHER made rival politicians hold hands and sing together at Basildon's St Luke's Hospice.

It happened at the annual dedication service in a marquee as the congregation stood to sing the folk hymn Bind Us Together Lord.

Laughter stopped the service when preacher the Rev Richard Davies said to Tory David Amess and Liberal Basildon Council chairman David Harrison: "Come on now, everyone has to hold hands while they sing this one."

The two politicians drew applause when they laughed and stood holding hands as they sang the hymn.

Close

Afterwards, when Mr Amess spoke to the congregation he thanked Mr Davies for bringing them to close together.

"But I don't think it's something we are going to do afterwards," he said.

He presented a cheque for £250 from the housing department of the Commission for New Towns and said: "Out of such a sad cause as the hospice it is remarkable that so many people have been brought together, and the community united."

When Mr Harrison handed over a cheque for £10,685, a record for a chairman's appeal, he said they hoped this

year would see the start of building, before costs soar.

"If a builder can be found to start before the other £200,000 is raised then I'm sure the community will be prepared to come up here and dig holes to help," he said.

Coun Harrison said he would like to continue with the appeal in the coming year and raise another £10,000.

It was this togetherness from everyone in our community that made Fun Days such a success.

Our services always had greetings brought by the representatives from Basildon Council, the Mayor of Thurrock and our MPs.

At the end of each Fun Day we came together, in the marquee in the hospice garden, for a special Thanksgiving Celebration led by our Hospice chaplain.

Here we were joined by our friends from churches in our catchment area accompanied by choirs and gifted musicians.

I've included the newspaper cutting as a 'fun way' of illustrating the 'family atmosphere' you will find at St. Luke's.

Counting all the Fun Day Pennies

Hands on the money

Following our Fun Days in Basildon Town Centre we were again guests at the police station, performing the happy task of counting all the money collected.

Altogether our Fun Days raised an enormous sum of money - thousands of pounds - which was a tremendous amount of money in those early days.

Thank you to everyone who helped us with our Fun Days

Our First Fundraising Groups

Earlier in the book I mentioned Minnie, my patient giving me the first 25p as a token to start the hospice.

Over the next few months Minnie's 'sitting room' turned into the first official Hospice Fundraising venue in Basildon.

After our first group in Basildon seven more fundraising groups were established.

As in Basildon, I found there were other groups of dedicated and committed people ready to take up the baton to support the building of St. Luke's.

Further groups began in Corringham, Wickford, Grays, South Ockendon, Billericay, Tilbury and our Special Events Group. Many of the groups still have founder members today who were there at the very begining of the hospice journey.

In the next few pages I go into more detail how the hospice fundraising Groups began and who the wonderful people were who came forward to help us at that time.

Of course, our Fundraising Groups are just a small but important part of the support St. Luke's receives.

Much of our help also came from the general public. Ordinary people wanted to raise money for us by doing their own events, either individually or in groups.

They also supported us in the special events our Fundraising Groups organised.

The programme on this page is for a Service of Thanksgiving we held at the Hospice for our Fundraising Groups in 1993. At that time we had been opened for Day Care for three years.

It shows the number of Fundraising Groups that had been created since the vision of a community hospice had been made public.

I'm always amazed at the staying power of a St. Luke's supporter. These people are truly fantastic.

And to think it had all started in Minnie's sitting room with her 25p.

I cannot thank all the dedicated and committed people who joined these groups and continued to support them and the hospice over many, many years. They made it possible for us to bring the vision to reality to this day.

As you are reading this, and if you would like to help St. Luke's, too, you are very welcome to join one of our Fundraising Groups.

If you contact the hospice they will give you all the necessary details.

We thank God for our groups and the members of our caring community who have supported us from the very early days and still do.

My thanks to you all. God bless you.

St. Luke's Hospice

| Basildon Fundraising Group | Grays Fundraising Group | Special Events Group | Corringham Fundraising Group | South Ockendon Fundraising Group |

Tilbury Fundraising Group

Billericay Fundraising Group

SERVICE OF THANSGIVING

FOR 10 YEARS OF FUNDRAISING

Wickford Fundraising Group

SUNDAY 25TH APRIL 1993

Stanford le Hope Fundraising Group

Fobbing Farm Nethermayne Basildon Essex SS16 5NJ

St. Luke's Fundraising Groups

Basildon & Langdon Hills Fundraising Group

First Fundraising Group - Basildon/Langdon Hills

Corringham & Stanford le Hope Fundraising Group

An early photo of the combined Corringham and Standford Group

The present Group members

The St. Luke's Basildon Fundraising Group was founded in 1983.

The first meetings were in Minnie's sitting room (as mentioned earlier it was Minnie, my patient, who gave us our first 25p token donation.).

The group expanded quite rapidly and grew to 24 members. For our monthly meetings we moved to Whitmore Court, the Community Hall for the Whitmore Way Estate in Basildon. As membership dropped, due to members moving away and others being physically unable to continue, the group joined with our Langdon Hills friends, combining two areas - Basildon and Langdon Hills. The combined group continues to meet each month on a Wednesday afternoon in the members homes. After 27 years two of the original members are still there helping to raise money for St. Luke's.

I first met Rita Rawlinson, founder of the Corringham Group, in one of my patient's homes when I visited as a District Nurse. The patient was suffering from cancer and desperately needed help.

All this happened soon after that fateful Christmas Eve when I felt God had called me to establish a home for cancer patients and their families. Soon Rita and her husband Dan's home was filled to the brim with jumble & bric-a-brac. Dan, a gifted artist, also allowed us to sell some of his work.

At the same time Gladys Bacon formed the Stanford le Hope Group meeting in her sitting room. This Group fundraised for many years. Following Gladys' death membership dwindled and the Stanford Group joined together with Corringham.

The combined Group now comprises 14 members and meet regularly at each other's homes to discuss and organise various events.

St. Luke's Fundraising Groups

Wickford Fundraising Group

An early photo of the Wickford Fundraising Grouup

Grays Fundraising Group

The Grays Convent Sisters.
Sister Anne is seated in the middle

Trevor Williams and I both worked as district Nurses in our area. Trevor also supported me in the field of continuous education and for a period was a member of the Hospice Management Team.

Trevor and his wife Jane started fundraising for us with their friends Laurie and Gwen Lay. Laurie and Gwen, like Trevor and Jane, were committed and active members of Christ Church in Wickford. These four became the founder members of the Hospice Wickford Fundraising Group and launched their group in 1989 with a public meeting at Christ Church.

Soon other caring folk from Wickford and members of Christ Church joined our original four. The church allowed the Group to meet on church premises free of charge. They now hold their meetings in each other's homes.

I met John and Jane Scowen in Grays and they agreed to establish a Fundraising Group. Both John and Jane had many other commitments as they were both talented singers. They eventually handed over the Group to Sister Anne Hanks from Grays Convent in 1990.

Sister Anne agreed to become the Fundraising Co-ordinator for Grays.

The Convent with its beautiful gardens and with the support from her fellow sisters soon engaged friends and members of their local community and St. Thomas School and Church.

They continued to meet at the Convent for their monthly meetings and held many fundraising events there.

An early picture of our fundraising group co-ordinators posing for the camera

St. Luke's Fundraising Groups

South Ockenden Fundraising Group

Betty Phillips' South Ockendon Group is one of our oldest. As soon as Betty heard of my plans of trying to establish a hospice in the area of Basildon, Billericay, Wickford and Thurrock she came to see me.

Betty, and her husband Mick's daughter, Lesley was a patient at The Royal Marsden Hospital. While Lesley was in the Royal Marsden she wrote a lovely book of poems.

Although I never got to know Lesley I felt I did know her through her poems. Betty and Mick had Lesley's poems printed and decided the proceeds from the sale of the book should be shared between St. Luke's and Cancer Research.

An early photo of Betty's Group with an inset picture of Betty's daughter, Lesley

Betty lives in South Ockendon and later with friends and neighbours founded the South Ockendon Fundraising Group and several events were held.

The actual group was small but it was amazing what they achieved.

When St. Luke's opened their Charity Shop in Derwent Parade, South Ockendon, Betty became its manager. She felt she could not continue as fundraising co-ordinator and manager of the shop at the same time. The group then folded but Betty being Betty took all her fundraising group members with her to help as volunteerss in the shop.

They work so hard and it was and is a real pleasure to see their smiling faces, enthusiasm, and love for St. Luke's when I visit their shop.

Tilbury Fundraising Group

The Tilbury Fundraising Group came into being solely through the enthusiasm and committment of Freda Finnerty.

I met Freda when I was selling 'symbolic' bricks to raise money for the building of St. Luke's.

Soon afterwards I gave a talk in Tilbury on the vision of a community hospice and Freda and I got to know each other better and became instant friends.

Freda, her daughters and grandchildren, together with their friends really got into the fundraising spirit.

We then decided to make the group official, to be known as Tilbury Fundraising Group with Freda as Co-ordinator and Father Tim, the local priest, as chairman.

Freda and friends get all dressed up for Dickensian Market at Basildon.

The group continued for several years. Sadly, Freda's daughter, became ill and the official Tilbury Fundraising group had to disband.

Although Freda now had extra family commitments her support and love for St. Luke's never stopped. She continued raising funds with the help of grandchildren, family and friends.

At the time of writing, Freda has finally retired from active fundraising but continues to support the Hospice whenever or wherever she can.

St. Luke's Fundraising Groups

Billericay Fundraising Group

As with most of the fundraising groups they started with one or two founder members and gradually enthused and encouraged others to join.

Janet Lees, from Billericay Methodist Church, and our own Bill Crafer are founder members of Billericay Group. They were soon joined by Richard Cook and his wife Anne. Richard took over the role of chairman for several years. When Richard retired as Chair, Doreen Fisher took on the role as Co-ordinator for the Billericay Group

Again, like the other established fundraising groups they are always looking forward to welcome more new members.

Anne & Richard Cook, with Doreen Fisher

*Magic Evening with Billericay fundraisers -
watch the cards closely !*

St. Luke's Events Group

The 'Events Group' was formed by Amanda Walsham and Kate Bouchet and their friends.

I first met Amanda and her husband John at their then South Ockendon Garden Centre, now known as Thurrock Garden Centre. An instant friendship was formed which has lasted all these years and they immediately offered to help and support St. Luke's.

It was in the early years. They were so kind and allowed us to have a stall with publicity items at the entrance of their garden centre.

We spent the whole weekend fundraising, with Amanda and John donating some shop items to sell and encouraging people to look at our 'Hospice Plans' and listening to the St. Luke's story.

Amanda, antiques expert David Batty, and Kate

Amanda then encouraged her business friends to form a fundraising group to be known as the 'Events Group' to organise large special events.

They organise two or three big showcase attrractions each year to really bring in the funds.

Our Fundraising Groups are always looking for new members. If you would like to join a very friendly group of committed people and have a lot of fun on the way please contact St. Luke's for details of your local group. I've listed a few of the kind of things you would get involved in... there are many, many more:

Fetes	Raffles	Magic Evenings	bric-a-brac stalls	Auctions	Bazaars	Making Knitted Items
Barbeques		Selling Hospice Merchandise	Wedding Shows		Making Home Made Jams	
Special Themed Meals		Fashions shows	Home Made Cards	Cream Teas		Jazz Concerts

---

Handicrafts Group And Trudy Goes To Jail

We were continously trying to raise funds for the Hospice and at the same time encouraging old and new friends to join us.

We wanted to re-establish a 'Handicraft Group',

A few of us met once a month at the hospice - learning from more gifted friends the intricacies of needlework and embroidery to produce gift items to sell.

We enjoyed a social evening together in the hospice dining room, using one of the large cupboards to store our craft ware, mainly embroidery silks, scraps of material, and our sewing machine. We gradually built up a good stock.

It was fun working together, encouraging one another and learning from each other.

The completed items would then be sold at our various fetes or sold privately to neighbours or friends.

As we all got older and some members became housebound, we discontinued meeting at the hospice, but our dear sewing and knitting friends continued meeting in their homes and have done so for many years.

They still make beautiful gifts for sale. They have stalls either in their street, at our annual fete, in the hospital, or wherever there is an opportunity to display their home made goods.

Thank you all so much for supporting St. Luke's in such a very faithful way.

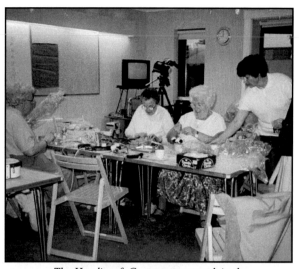

The Handicraft Group gets to work in the hospice dining room

The result of many hours of work by nimble fingers

Trudy goes to jail.

If you remember from earlier in my story I told you how Bill Crafer was having a paddle in Eastgate Shopping Centre.

Well, while he was enjoying himself with his bucket and spade, Dr Jean Maxwell, Day Care Sister Viv's husband Ray and I, were locked up in Chelmsford jail.

It was all for charity I hasten to add - a sponsored jail break for St. Luke's.

We had to escape out of the prison and get as far away as we could without spending any money. We managed to reach Jersey by courtesy of a free flight from Southend airport.

The three jailbreakers hide in the bushes

Our escape to the Channel Islands coincided with the national Voices for Hospices appeal.

We ended up being guests of honour at the local Jersey Hospice and joined in their concert.

They also allowed us to stay there overnight on some make-shift beds.

It was great fun, especially when the other passengers saw us board the plane.

Hospice Charity Shops

Earlier in the book you may remember the photographs of Margaret and Doris pushing their pram loaded up with bric-a-brac. They were on their way to Whitmore Community Hall to try to raise money for the hospice by selling their goods.

One of our selling premises was a doctor's surgery in the Fremnells, Basildon. A good friend of mine, Dr. Suzy, allowed us to store items for sale in a shed at the side of her surgery rooms. At weekends and whenever we had an opportunity to borrow a hall free of charge Margaret and Doris collected the items from the shed in Margaret's pram.

Margaret outside her Fremnells' 'shop' with Dr. Suzy inset

Sadly, following Dr. Suzy's sudden and untimely death, the surgery was closed down. With our earlier connections with Suzy we were eventually able to persuade the powers that be to let us have the premises as a store-room and selling outlet. Later Margaret converted the space into a temporary shop.

We knew this is what Suzy would have wanted as for many years she had been a staunch supporter of our vision for a home for cancer patients and their families. She even opened her own home up for us to hold functions.

Our Liberty Hall shop with staff

From that first small step with the pram filled with bric a brac from our flea market stall to jumble sales, we started our journey into the retail business. 1991 was a very special time for all of us. How excited we were when we were officially registered at Companies House - SLH Trading Ltd - with Les, my husband, in charge as director. We moved into our very first 'proper shop' in the Galleries at Eastgate Shopping Centre. Before long we outgrew this and moved to a new site at Liberty Hall in Basildon.

At this time Jean Edwards, one of our early volunteers, was appointed as shops manager and co-ordinator. Les and Jean managed to secure our next shop in Broxburn Road, South Ockendon.

Jean Edwards our first shops manager

Betty Phillips was the first manager here before being transferred to our second shop in South Ockendon, at Derwent Parade.

We also have a warehouse where all donated items are stored: clothes, bric a brac and books to larger items like furniture. They are sorted, cleaned and valued by our dedicated volunteers. Those which cannot be sold are re-cycled. Electrical goods are checked by a qualified electrician to make sure they are safe.

Donated goods being checked in our warehouse

Hospice Charity Shops

Our hospice vans, their drivers and crews, are well known throughout our area distributing the goods from the warehouse to our shops. They are also available for house clearances.

"You hum it, Norman, I'll play it"

Long serving volunteer driver Norman with one of our hospice vans

Our distinctive shop sign

One by one more shops have opened. At the time of writing this book St Luke's has a total of ten charity shops.

In each area they have become a part of local community life, information centres and focus points for people wanting to know more about the hospice and how to support St. Luke's.

We are, of course, very fortunate to live in a community of generous people who have done and continue to this day donating items for sale.

I am often amazed by the quality and variety of the goods donated to us.

Thank you very, very much.

The expansion of our retail shops has only been possible because of our dedicated staff and volunteers. They never seem to tire in their enthusiasm and commitment to St. Luke's, by sharing their skills, talent and time.

The work continues as it must and to this day all the staff and volunteers associated with SLH Trading work hard to raise money so that our patients and their families receive the best care possible when they need it most.

The warm and welcoming atmosphere in our shops mirrors the hospice ethos of the 'family feeling' we have at St. Luke's into our wider community.

Planning of Building Works - Phase II

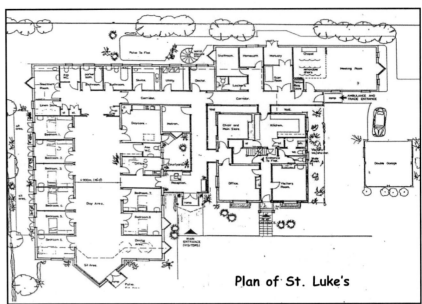

The Hospice Management Committee with our architect, quantity surveyor and structural engineer held many meetings prior to commencement of the building work for phase II.

Following my poor attempt of a 'dream' drawing of the new Day Care and In-Patient unit, Peter presented us with his professional version.

Plan of St. Luke's

Peter with the town planner

JOHN STRONG & PARTNERS
Chartered Architects   88a High Street Billericay Essex CMI2 9BT

Telephone 027 74 3101/2

20 June 1985

Mr. & Mrs. L. Cox

With Compliments   Regards - Peter.

Trudy with the town planner

Following these initial meetings we then invited members of the Health Authority, Fire Brigade and representatives from the Council Planning Dept making absolutely sure that all guidelines were followed and adhered to.

Building Work - Phase II Begins

Finally the long awaiting day came when the actual building work could begin.

How excited we all were.

Our photo show our MPs -Tim Jarman (Thurrock), David Amess (Basildon), Architect Peter Strong and myself as the first stake is driven in. David is wielding the big hammer while Tim 'bravely' held the stake.

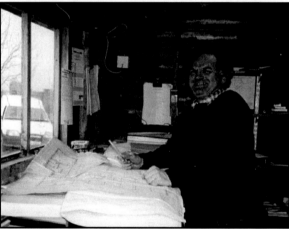

Here was the result of all the hard work of so many people raising funds over the past seven years finally taking shape; all under the watchful eye of Ray, our site foreman.

WORK began yesterday on Basildon's long-awaited hospice extension.

Basildon and Thurrock MPs David Amess and Tim Janman were there to lend a hand at the Fobbing Farm site on an occasion that turned dream into reality.

Mr Amess is seen wielding a sledge hammer to a peg held by Mr Janman, as hospice matron Trudy Cox and others look on.

☐ ☐

Five years of fund raising have gone into making St Luke's Hospice possible — and there is still a long way to go.

The new building, which will take 26 weeks to finish, will comprise an eight bed unit, a day care centre and a children's play area.

Sister Cox said: "It is just dawning on me that this is really it, because there have been so many times when we thought we were just about there and then there have been delays."

Fobbing Farm House was bought by the hospice appeal and in April 1985 a dedication service was held to mark the official start of the conversion programme, which was completed in September 1986.

It is now used as the administrative headquarters of the appeal and is also the Cox family home.

☐ ☐

The charity has enough money to finish the buildings, but it still needs £200,000 to fit them out and staff them.

Mrs Cox said: "We are serving over 300,000 people. If everybody gave just £1, we would have no problem and could finish the building and start work in a year."

Her dream of opening the hospice began five years ago and since then £700,000 has been raised.

The hospice already has a team of

Hospice dream moves close to reality

volunteers trained to provide a round-the clock sitting service for cancer victims at home, as well as a bereavement service, with trained volunteers.

When the building is finished, the hospice will have eight beds for in patients, a day care unit and the home support service.

☐ ☐

Hospice publicity manager David McIntyre said: "1989 is the year of the big push. We have a new incentive to drive for the finish.

"This year is bringing the dream nearer reality. Hopefully, some time next year the dream of patients will come true."

The hospice covers the area of Basildon and Thurrock District Health Authority and is funded entirely by charity.

It ran into problems because new regulations from the European Court meant it had to pay VAT on the new buildings.

If the hospice runs out of money, the building will have to stop.

Mr McIntyre said: "You have got to keep reminding people that the money is needed."

Mud - Mud - Mud ...

It was all a bit like the famous hippotamus song. "Mud, Mud, glorious Mud.... as the diggers and bulldozers got to work. But we were so happy to get started at last we didn't mind the mess !

Once the foundations had been concreted we were ready to continue with the building of walls for both units - Day Care and In-Patients - but we had run out of money.

Our financial situation was such that we did not have enough money to cover the building costs or continue.

It warranted a further visit to the hospital and a meeting with Richard, the Chief Executive.

Richard arranged for me to see Ken, Director of Finance, in the hope of getting an interest free loan to continue with the building work.

Thanks to their generous interest free loan we were able to continue with building the hospice.

Next - The Foundations

The Building work started up again.

We were so fortunate to have Frank, who took over the reponsibility of Clerk of Works.

My photograph shows him inspecting the foundation of the dining/meeting room.

Of course, I couldn't resist sliding down the sand hills.

The Roof Timbers Arrive

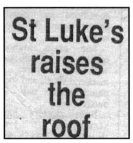

The photograph above is of the In-Patient Unit looking towards the bay area and the one below of the pipework laid below the floors.

This photo shows the roof trusses housing the water tanks before the walls and ceilings were put it. How different it all looks now !

Of course, Gerry, our accountant at that time, is now our present Chairman of the Hospice Trustees. He wanted to make sure the brickwork and building work were up to scratch.

The Final Touches

The final touches always take the most time, don't they? Later came the decoration and furnishing of all the rooms, but, first, we needed to establish the car park and grounds.

That will be really great, as we, as a family, seemed to have been living in wellington boots to cope with the mud.

It's definitely not easy having a jumble sale on a building site.

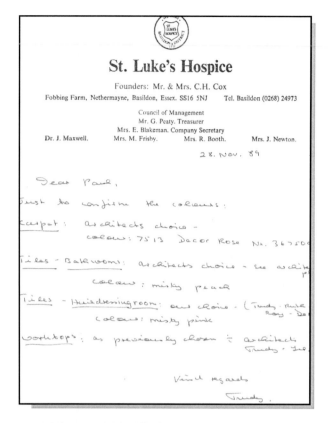

In the meantime our friend, Ted, was busy painting the kitchen in the upstairs flat. Thank you, Ted, for making our kitchen look nice again.

Decisions now had to be made regarding ordering carpets, what colour was to go where, picking the right wallpaper, deciding on the right colour schemes, etc, -- not an easy task.

Meanwhile, Bill Crafer, was making some last minute alterations in the boiler house.

Doesn't it look complicated ?

As for our family we were seeing our dream come true - a new hospice being built before our eyes - or in this photo mine and the eyes of my son Michael and his two girls, Danielle and Nicola.

The Final, Final Touches

Last minute instructions from Les

As the final countdown begins, Frank, our voluntary Clerk of Works, makes a last minute check over the plans to make sure the builders haven't missed anything.

Les had some final instructions for the builders.

The workforce enjoy that good old British tradition of a cup of tea in the sun.

It's now time for Les to open the bottle of bubbly.

We've made it !!

Our work force deserve their a well earned break

The Ceremony Of The Keys - Hospice Style

The great day arrived. St Luke's had been built.

It had taken seven years hard fundraising by our truly wonderful community of Thurrock, Basildon, Billiericay and Wickford, supporting us every step of the way.

I'm not ashamed to admit a little bitty tear was shed on the day I had the keys in my hand.

Now we were ready to receive our nursing staff and our first patients.

It was the start of a different phase in the life of the hospice.

Getting The Unit Ready

When the building work was finished on the house and the unit extension, our sparkling new hospice was ready.

Of course, it was just a bare empty shell but we now had the happy task of bringing it to life. Putting into place all the necessary bits and pieces needed to get St. Luke's ready for our proposed Open Days and welcoming our first Day Care patient.

Beds, chairs. tables; curtains, cushions, trolleys, cooking pots and pans; all our office equipment; books, papers, telephones and desks. You could say everything except the kitchen sink but only because that was already there!

It was hard work but also great fun and once again we were blessed with a great team of volunteers, family and friends who all put their shoulders to the 'Hospice Wheel' and made everything just perfect. Our collection of photographs of our 'moving in' will hopefully illustrate how we made St. Luke's come alive.

First, the all important beds arrive to be pushed into the hospice.

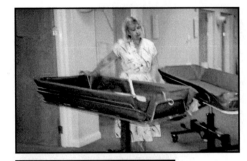

While Staff Nurse Jenni is checking out the shower trollies and sorting out the mattresses,

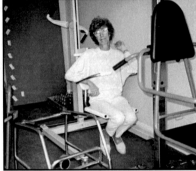

Stella is busy trying out the hoist and appears to be really enjoying it.

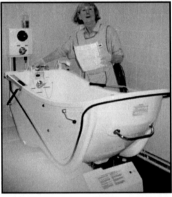

Hilary admiring the new 'sit in bath' and trying to learn how the jacuzzi works while the curtain makers get to work.

Getting The Unit Ready ...

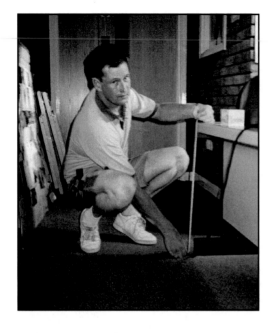

Choosing and sewing the curtains, fixing the rails and hanging the curtains soon fills the Unit with a homely touch.

Above our dear friend, Ray, our carpenter, is busy measuring. He made all the bedroom furniture, wardrobes, bedside cabinets, tea bar and wherever we needed shelving in the Unit.

The Two Bills.

While Bill Crafer (left) is busy drilling for shelving and other fixtures in the bathroom and sluice area, his staunch helper, Bill Brown, was keeping a watchful eye on the meters in the basement.

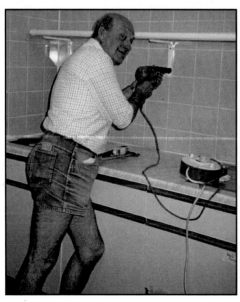

Getting The Unit Ready ...

Of course, there were a hundred and one things to do, some very basic tasks, like cleaning windows and tidying up the office but still very important before we welcomed our first patient.

Brenda and friend are busy shining the glass while Barbara is soon knocking the office into shape, (how did it get into such a mess?).

Kathy, meanwhile, is happy in her new kitchen sorting out the cutlery and joining Hilda and Maud guarding the chain rope -- nobody is allowed to see the kitchen until it is spic and span !

Getting The Unit Ready ...

* Julia getting the posters and display boards ready

* Ruth and Lee were kept busy emptying all the many boxes;

* Les was hard at work 'supervised' by son, Christopher;

* Sue and Jenni were sorting out all the chairs in the chapel area;

* The beds and armchairs were in an untidy pile in the middle of the unit;

* I had a trolley full of boxes, trays, and files I had to find a home for;

* Would we be ready in time ?

Well, we still have one more page to show you but then you will find out the answer !

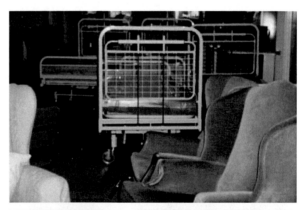

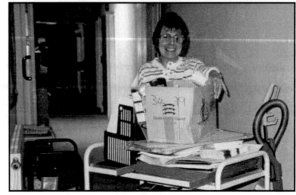

Getting The Unit Ready ...

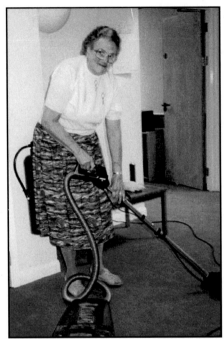

Elsie gets cracking with the hoover while Chris makes all the beautiful room number tiles.

Peter and friends put the finishing touches to the courtyard benches.

Myself, Sister Viv, and Staff Nurse Jenni reading one of the many messages of good wishes for St. Luke's and everyone connected with the vision.

Everyone had worked so hard raising the necessary funds and then helping to make sure everything was perfect as we opened our doors and welcomed our first Day Care patient.

I cannot begin to thank all the many people involved in my dream but I was so happy that day when it all came true.

We Hold Open Days

Once the unit was completed we were ready for our "open days" at the hospice.

So many people came, - individuals as well as organisations, from churches and schools, clubs in our area. Everyone was now eager to see and hear what had been achieved with their help.

A few of us, Ruth, Bill, Jennie, Sue and myself proudly showed our visitors around and explained about the work of the hospice, the needs our patients and their families had.

We encouraged schools to hold a competition designing posters. We stuck 'paper bubbles' on the wall showing the cost of various items, such as furnishings required.

Our visitors were invited to donate whatever was needed and whatever they could afford. Many more donations were received during these tours to help complete the last necessary and special items needed.

So gradually the bedrooms were filled with beds, lights, furniture and other necessary items.

95

Open Days

To St Lukes Hospice

I hope you raised a Lot of money and equipment. I hope you are pleased with my savings.

Lots of Love

Lucy. xx
age 8

The community once again made us proud to be part of them. They were so generous, old and young contributed.

We will never be able to thank all of you enough for helping us to furnish the hospice. Office equipment was donated by Carsons, the office supply factory.

Marks & Spencer equipped our hairdressing and beauty salon to name just two of local firms who helped.

Open Days

Steven's family donated a bath with a door, including a jacussi. Steven died very young, suffering from cancer. The family organised fundraising events to buy this beautiful bath.

They also donated the 'chalet', known as 'Steven's Chalet'. It was again donated in memory of their dear son.

As our chalet from Clay Hill Road was much smaller we used Steven's Chalet as our future 'tea room', during our many jumble sales at the hospice.

One of our first official visitors who joined us for a 'trial meal' were our dear friends from Fair Haven Hospice in Southend.

Daphne, the matron there, and Ken, Administrator, had supported both Les and myself for many years. Their friendship, encouragement, advice and love to us both will never be forgotten.

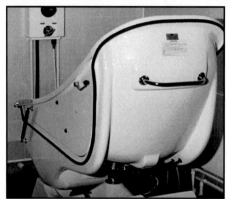

Open Day at St. Luke's

97

The Miracle of the Saucepans

There have been many miracles in the building and the working of St. Luke's.

The one I would like to tell you about here is the 'Miracle of the Saucepans'

A few days before we were expecting our first day Care patient everything was more or less ready.

There was only one problem - we needed more saucepans and other catering equipment.

I asked everyone if they could spare some saucepans to help us out. I also knew I had some new saucepans sitting upstairs in my kitchen but I really wanted to keep them for myself.

We had never had much money, always enough to live on, but not for luxuries. But the saucepans I had saved up for and eventually bought for us as a family were very expensive.

They looked so nice and shiny in our kitchen. The strange thing was I don't even like cooking very much but I loved my new saucepans.

After battling with myself over this for a few days I told myself I was being very selfish asking everyone else to donate their saucepans but I was not prepared to do it myself. I finally decided my saucepans should go downstairs to the hospice.

I felt much better, after that. I had asked everyone else to part with theirs, so why not me?.

The very next day there was a knock on the door. Someone had delivered two large boxes for the hospice.

As I opened them, there before my eyes, were a brand spanking new set of saucepans, baking dishes and trays, pans, tea and coffee pots and other catering utensils, still all wrapped in plastic coverings. They had never been used.

I just couldn't believe it. I sat there. I was so ashamed and so excited all at the same time. I had to be prepared

to part with my saucepans and then, once again as so often in the hospice story, God provided through some very, very kind people.

I later learned that the donors had no idea that's what we urgently needed. The person who sent them to us had had them in his garage for a few years and he in turn had been given them from someone who used to be a representative for a catering firm.

Many years later, at a carers support meeting, I met the man from whom the saucepans had come originally.

So another miracle, The Miracle of the Saucepans, was added to the many we have experienced at the hospice.

We were now ready for our first Day Care patient.

Hospice -- 'just like home'

Hospice? It's just like home

By ANN WRIGHT

HUNDREDS flocked to see the long-awaited St Luke's Hospice when it opened its doors for a preview this weekend.

The Basildon hospice, inspired by Sister Trudy Cox, is ready for business after seven years of frantic fund raising, but cannot open until £160,000 more has been raised to pay back a loan for the building.

Guided tours were laid on throughout the weekend and there was a thanksgiving service on Saturday afternoon.

A garden party was held in the grounds of the neighbouring sports centre with pony rides, cream teas, raffles, and stalls.

Exhibitions explained how the hospice was born, and each room was costed out so visitors could see where the money went.

Sister Cox said: "The public has been invited to come

community for the community."

She hopes to admit the first patients in the spring, although the first day-patients arrived at the beginning of June.

She said: "The first patient, when she entered, said 'Oh, it is just like home', and that was music to my ears.

"It made the seven years of hard work and fund raising worth while. It was the image we wanted, to make a home for people who need it.

"The patients cannot come in until we get the money, and we are asking firms to adopt the pay roll giving scheme, £1 a month dedicated from the salary is less then

fully operation by next spring — unless a miracle happens.

Sister Cox said: "It is lovely everybody being here, but we do need money. I feel embarrassed always asking for money but somebody has to do it.

"I only overcome my embarrassment by thinking of a particular patient."

So far she has raised £700,000 from the first donation of 25 pence which is proudly displayed in the hospice.

The gardens are being landscaped and Sister Cox hopes to introduce an adopt a plot scheme for people to tend them.

She also appealed for people to bake cakes for the day-patients, and to buy small gifts of food or provisions to help the hospice.

- It is open on Wednesday

Hospice Administrator Les, Finance Assistant Bill, and his wife, Barbara, Volunteer Co-ordinator, adding the final touches. My other photos, top to bottom, show the dining room, bay area, and patient room, and myself, ready for the arrival of our first patient.

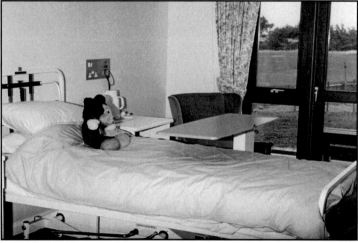

Our First Day Care Patient Arrives

The most important date in the Hospice Calendar was the 5th June 1990.

There were smiles all around on that day - the day when we were finally ready to receive our first Day Care patient.

Hospice? It's just like home

This was the headline in the local press reporting the opening of St. Luke's

When Joan, our first Day Care patient, arrived at the hospice -- like most of our patients she was very apprehensive - 'would it be a sad place' - was one of those doubts on her lips.

The word 'Hospice' even to this day still puts fear into people.

Sister Viv welcomes Joan to the Hospice

But as Jean entered and was given a warm 'hospice welcome hug', she looked around, stopped and turned to us and said, "Oh it's just like being at home".

It was wonderful to hear her say that.

Even if we had briefed her she could not have given us, and especially me, more reassurance that we needed.

We do not want to replace "home" but strive to make St. Luke's as homely as possible.

Jenni, Jean and Viv ready for the big day

We try to make it a place of living every day to the full while not ignoring the needs of our patients and their physical well being.

We endeavour to help with their emotional needs, their social worries and spiritual concerns and Love and support them the best way we know how.

Viv Waters, who had worked as a District Nurse for many years, was appointed as the Day Care Sister.

We had both worked together as District Nursing Sisters for many years and had become great friends.

Jenni Newton, who was a member of our Management Committee was appointed as Staff Nurse for Day Care.

Jenni had previously worked at St Andrews Hospital, Billericay, in the Burns Unit.

Dr. Jean Maxwell, was a GP at Basildon and a member of the Management Committee. Jean took on the role of volunteer Day Care doctor.

We were so grateful to Jean, who visited the hospice regularly, as well as being on call if we ever needed her advice in an emergency. Thank you, Jean, so much.

We were all very excited but also a little nervous when the day finally arrived to welcome our very first patient.

For me the responsibilty of the opening of the hospice hit me very hard. Will I be good enough for the task ahead; to make sure that we do the very best for our patients and their families? Please, God, help me.

Day Care At St. Luke's

Trudy with Joan

'What could be better than a nice cup of tea'. Staff Nurse Jenni and Sister Viv make sure Joan is ok

All my life I suffered from a lack of confidence and those who really know me are aware of that. I am basically a happy, cheerful person and managed to cover it up well but I knew that God had given me the vision of a place to care for patients and their families.

I also knew that He will care for me. I prayed hard for guidance, wisdom, health and strength and when the patient arrived I felt very much at peace, knowing that is what the vision was all about.

Soon other patients joined Joan. St. Luke's with its happy family atmosphere really came to life.

It is wonderful to see the faces of our patients, so anxious when they first arrive but soon more relaxed and enjoying each other's company. They were soon making friends, sharing meals, enjoying the entertainment provided and appreciating that our staff had time for them.

Our staff to patient ratio is high and that is the difference between hospital and hospice.

Hospitals are such busy places and a great demand is made on all the staff. They're caring and compassionate nurses, that is why they joined the profession, but fewer in numbers and under much more time pressure than we are.

We, at the hospice, are very privileged. And, of course, we are so blessed with our volunteers.

They bring so many talents, from hairdressing to manicuring; from flower arranging to organising quizzes and assisting the trained staff whenever they need a hand.

Every day one of our Chaplaincy Team visits our patients and if they wish to have a chat, they have that opportunity.

Some patients ask for a special hymn to be sung at our short daily services or a special prayer or chat with them about families and other concerns within the confines of confidentiality.

Before being able to join the staff as volunteers everyone had to attend a volunteer course and further training sessions depending which area of work they are in and all are bound to confidentiality.

Our patients are aware that we are very strict in this matter and therefore feel safe.

The patients are always very pleased when Dr. Jean pops in making sure all is well.

We are so grateful to Jean for giving us, staff as well as patients her precious time.

To us as nurses it is very reassuring to know that a doctor is at hand when needed.

Apart from having a chat with Dr. Jean, patients also have an opportunity to talk to our Social Worker, see a Therapist, Physiotherapist or any nursing care required.

Day Care is very much about living life to the full and St. Luke's is there to help achieve this.

Our patients can take part in a whole range of activities from quizzes, handicrafts and artistic pursuits, musical and themed days, days out at the seaside, restaurant outings and visits to various local gardens and historical houses.

But, importantly there is a serious caring side to it, too.

Various therapies are on hand for Day Car patients from our nurses and volunteers.

Day Care At St. Luke's

A range of complementary therapies, such as, Reflexology, Aromotherapy and various treatments are available.

Day Care means 'Time For You'. There is always time to discuss problems; it may be concerning distressing symptoms, or needing reassurance with other difficulties.

Patients may require additional aids or equipment at home to make life a little easier for patients, as well as, the carer.

They may have financial burdens, housing issues, or social issues. Our Social Worker is at hand to help and advise. There may be various benefits they are entitled to which they are unaware.

Looking at these pictures and seeing the patient so relaxed and content makes me very pleased of the success of our Day Care Unit.

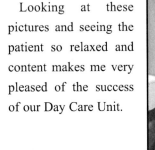

Our hospice cooks find out what our patients would like for dinner

Knitting or a chat with friends is just what the doctor ordered

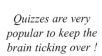

Quizzes are very popular to keep the brain ticking over !

A friendly cuppa and a chat with the Hospice Chaplain is always welcome

Our Day Care patients are very keen to keep everything in the courtyard looking lovely

Sister Viv presents a patient with a birthday cake

On the next couple of pages are a selection of our photographs which will hopefully give the reader a flavour of our Day Care facilities.

Day Care At St. Luke's

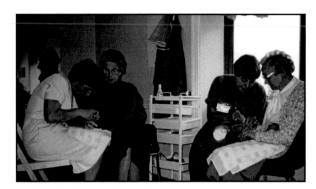

Nails are given a good polish

Day Care's drum wizard shows his skills at the skins

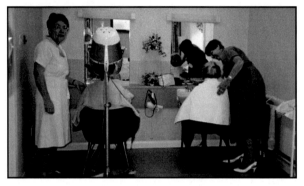

Hairdressing in a very professional looking hospice 'salon'

A 'shampoo and set' - certainly madam

Delicate work needs steady hands and nimble fingers

Painting can be a very messy business

Accordionist Bill entertains

A word of comfort from Hospice Chaplain, John

Day Care At St. Luke's

It's a tricky decision - making the best move

It's 'Teddies at the Ready' for this activity

*It looks like a rehearsal is in progress
for the Christmas Carols concert*

Who let that St. Trinian's lass in ?

*The children of Swan Mead School, Basildon, have always been great supporters of St. Lukes.
Here they are performing a play at Christmas Time for the Day Care patients*

*Day Care Christmas Lunch - with all the trimmings.
The staff and volunteers dress up in costumes to make it a meal to remember*

Day Care At St. Luke's

Animals play an important part in many peoples' lives and Day Care patients are no exception. Here are a selection of dogs and ponies who have visited St. Luke's and made friends with our patients.

  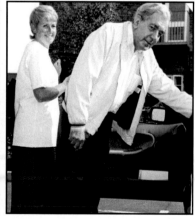

A very essential volunteer role in the care of our Day Care patients is that of a driver. Without these dedicated car drivers many of the patients would not be able to attend the Day Care Unit.

Duchess of Norfolk officially opens St. Luke's - What The Papers Said

Time for celebration as Duchess opens

St Luke's Hospice Day Care Centre

Opening of Luke's Hospice Day Care Centre

DREAM COMES TRUE

**Words: Maxine Ashford
Pictures: David Higgleton**

TRUDY COX, the driving force behind St Luke's Hospice received the best birthday present of her life this week — the official opening of the hospice day care centre.

Her Grace the Duchess of Norfolk, wearing a pale blue suit, arrived at the hospice on Wednesday morning amid jubilant cheers from infants and juniors representing schools all across the district.

With background music from the Essex Police Band and escort by the Basildon Blue Shadow Majorettes, the Duchess took time to stop and speak to many of the youngsters waiting patiently in the glorious sunshine.

Ten-year-old Cheryl Martin, of Basildon's Elmbrook school, who is confined to a wheelchair, was asked her age and the Duchess made a special point of saying how pretty she was.

And it was a day Nicky Portway, aged 10, will never forget.

He bravely presented a colourful pot plant to the Duchess on behalf of Jane Duke school, Markhams Chase, Basildon.

"I was really nervous, but the Duchess was so nice. She thanked me for the flowers and asked how we had helped raise money for the hospice," he said.

The Duchess, accompanied by Trudy Cox and hospice administrator Les Cox, her husband, was then entertained by the Basildon Youth Orchestra and school choirs, before the speeches and official opening ceremony took place.

But the day really belonged to Trudy, celebrating her 54th birthday.

She said: "It really is the best birthday present I have ever had.

"It has all been so tremendous that I am almost lost for words.

"During the seven years of work for the hospice, I never lost faith and knew this day would come, but I didn't realise God worked this slowly."

A total of £830,000 has been raised for the hospice so far, and as soon as the £126,000 of debts are paid off, the residential unit can be opened.

This sunshine day for them all to treasure

HER GRACE The Duchess of Norfolk, founder of Help the Hospices, delighted hundreds of waiting youngsters last Wednesday when she opened the Day Care

finally rewarded for all her hard work.

Celebrating her 54th birthday, she escorted the Duchess round St Luke's in bright sunshine, giving her a guided tour of the Day

The pages may have faded but the memories of that day are still crystal clear as if it was yesterday

Duchess of Norfolk Officially Opens Hospice

There are so many highlights in this wonderful story that it is difficult to choose.

One of them had to be our official opening of St. Luke's.

We had the great privilege and honour to have the Duchess of Norfolk for the official opening of St. Luke's Hospice.

I initially contacted her at Help the Hospices office in London and felt very nervous as I had never met a Duchess before.

She was a charming, kind lady. I felt so at ease when I met her. She was so interested in 'how it all came about and happened'.

I, of course, was full of enthusiasm in telling her the wonderful miracle of St. Luke's.

A miracle it is and always will be to me. I told her about my work as a District Nurse, my patient Minnie and the 25p. How the community in our area got together and helped in so many ways to make it all possible (In earlier chapters I told the story in more detail).

The Duchess was so interested and said that she would be delighted to come and share that happy occasion with us.

I met Her Grace once more at Kings Cross station where I joined her collecting for the charity, 'Help The Hospices'. The Duchess is the founder and president of this national charity to suport all hospices.

There was great excitement among patients and staff alike when I returned from London.

The whole hospice was in a buzz and the detailed planning began.

Organising this special event was quite a task but we were so fortunate to again have lots of help and support.

Cllr Geoff Williams, from the Basildon Choral Society and Ken Sharp, Director of Finance, Basildon and Thurrock Health Authority agreed to direct and control the comings and goings.

Police were involved with safety issues together with council members of both Thurrock and Basildon.

The unit changed out of all recognition for half was to be where we were going to hold a service of Thanksgiving and Dedication.

Her Grace Arrives

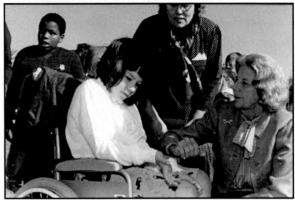

In the bay area our patients were waiting excitedly.

Prior to leaving the hospice to collect Her Grace the children practised their songs in the Unit.

The Mayor of Thurrock kindly lent us the official car with chauffeur and off I went to meet the Duchess at Basildon railway station with a lovely donated bunch of flowers.

She came on her own and looked just like an ordinary traveller but I had briefed the railway staff, who kindly escorted her and

me to our waiting official Mayor's car with chauffeur.

As we reached the Hospice - the Duchess was amazed to see so many children waving flags and banners.

The children all laughed and shouted, and tried to catch her attention and touch her.

It was so heart-warming the way she greeted them with great affection and the odd cuddle.

It took 20 minutes before we reached the Hospice car-park, which was a car-park no longer.

It was totally transformed. The bands, Police and Salvation Army, played to welcome her as well as a display by a Drum and Majorettes.

Her Grace Arrives

The youth orchestra played a welcome. One of the members of the orchestra was Kathy, daughter of our Day Care Sister Viv. She was playing the violin. Basildon Choral Society greeted them with hymns and choruses. The Essex Police Band were also in attendance and entertained us.

Children from Swan Mead and other local schools sang, all in their Sunday best with smiles all over their dear little faces. The schools' choir was conducted by Swan Mead's music teacher Jean Barnes, my good friend and supporter for many years.

Hundreds more children, patients and staff and volunteers, friends and family all welcomed her. Before actually entering the hospice we had all the official welcomes.

First, the Duchess was introduced to the two men mainly responsible for the planning and organising of the day's events, Cllr Geoff Williams and Basildon and Thurrock Authority Finance Director, Ken Sharp.

Our official photographs followed with the Duchess of Norfolk joining the line-up of myself and Les, the Mayor of Thurrock and the Chairman of Basildon Council.

Her Grace Arrives

It was then time to meet some of the very large crowd gathered at the Hospice.

I hope you will forgive me for including these two personal photographs but they are still very much part of the Hospice story. Without the support of Les and our three boys and their tolerance sharing their parents with everyone the Hospice would not have happened.

The pictures are of two of my grand-daughters, Danielle and Nicola, with Kirsty, our dear Stella's grand-daughter in the middle.

Danielle and Kirsty later presented bouquets to the Duchess. Pictured are my sons Christopher and Michael with Yvonne, Michael's wife.

As we walked up the path to the main entrance our kitchen volunteers and staff together with everyone around them sang a birthday song to me as the date was the 26th September, my birthday.

Naturally me being me, my tears flowed freely. But they were happy tears. I was surrounded by so much love.

As a bonus even the Duchess joined in, well, what a birthday.

Inside the Hospice the Duchess was introduced to the

Mayor of Thurrock and Chairman of Basildon Council, and our MP at that time, David Amess.

There then followed a short service of Thanksgiving and Dedication thanking God for his blessing and for sending all these lovely people to help, support and make everything possible. God works through people.

Duchess of Norfolk OpensThe Hospice

Speeches of welcome and greetings followed from the Duchesss of Norfolk; the Mayor of Thurrock; the Chair of Basildon Council, and David Amess, the Basildon MP and great supporter to me, personally and to St. We were now ready for the moment we had all strived and worked for. The unveiling of the plaque bringing smiles to everyone's faces.

Her Grace officially opens St. Luke's by unveiling the plaque.

Danielle (left) and Kirsty presented the Duchess of Norfolk with a bouquet.

Her Grace Meets Patients And My Family

Then, cakes and lots of chatter followed, while the Duchess met with our patients who were so thrilled meeting with this lovely, gracious lady.

The Duchess ended up spending half a day with us. It was wonderful. Her visit on that memorable day lasted for a total of five hours.

She took time (that precious commodity), to speak to patients, staff and volunteers and was genuinely interested in all that we told her.

For me, personally, the extra bonus was that my dear patients (for some it turned out to be their last visit to St. Luke's), and my family were with us celebrating not only my birthday but also the official opening of St. Luke's.

My father, Friedrich, with my mother, had travelled from his home in Germany for the opening. They met the Duchess, as did my sister Gisela, (holding baby Nicola), my sister-in-law Ingrid and my brother Herbert.

My other sister, Irmgard, who came to London to train as nurse like I did all those years ago, met the Duchess, too.

Her Grace Ends Her Visit To St. Luke's

I was very pleased about that because, more than anyone, Irmgard had been a great supporter of my vision for a hospice and was always there for me when problems or difficulties arose.

The Duchess also met two of my sons, Michael and Christopher. It had been quite a day for Nicola and Danielle, (Michael's daughters) and Kirsty.

Not only had they met a real live Duchess but Kirsty and Danielle had presented bouquets and shaken hands with her too. They deserved to relax and put their feet up.

I would like to explain the reason for this symbolic cheque present by the manager of MB Marquees to the Duchess.

This donation covered the cost of hiring and the labour involved in erecting the marquee. In effect it meant they allowed us to have their marquee for nothing.

Before the Duchess left for Basildon Station and home to London we had the first edition of the local paper, the Evening Echo, delivered.

We all had great fun, which Her Grace joined in, reading all about what had happened to St. Luke's during our opening day.

About 4pm our driver took us back to the station.

The Duchess, laden with presents, flowers and the newspaper as well as cakes for the journey from our Kathy, set off for home.

Letters From Her Grace

A few days later I received this letter from the
Duchess thanking us all for the wonderful visit.

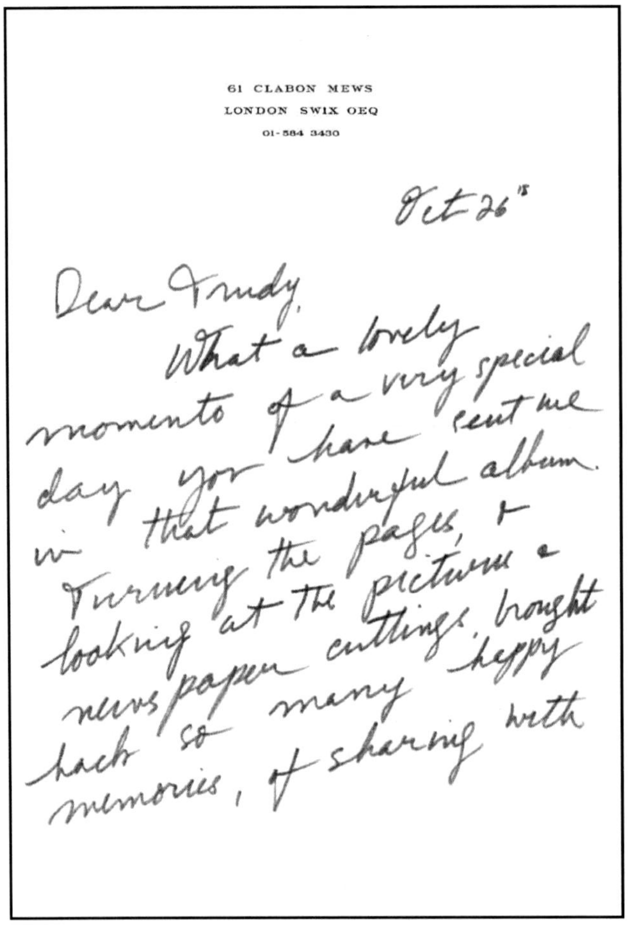

61 CLABON MEWS
LONDON SW1X OEQ
01-584 3430

Oct 26th

Dear Trudy,

What a lovely momento of a very special day you have sent me in that wonderful album. Turning the pages, & looking at the pictures & newspaper cuttings, brought back so many happy memories, & sharing with you that momentus occasion when all your hard work became a reality. As you yourself said, it was the best birthday present you could ever have had - and one that is going to bring hope & comfort to so many, & many people. Please thank all your staff for their wonderful welcome & thank you again for the momento of that great day.

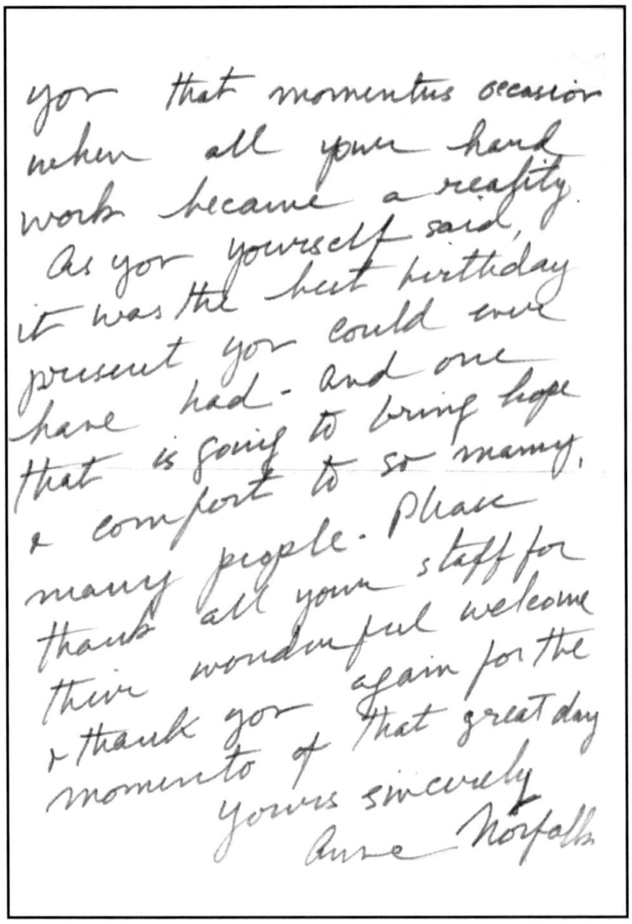

Yours sincerely
Anne Norfolk

*Thank you, your Grace, for making
this day so special for all of us*

114

Duchess Opens St. Luke's
What The Papers Said

Red carpet treatment amazes the Duchess

THE Duchess of Norfolk had never had such a welcome. When she opened the day care centre at Basildon's St Luke's Hospice yesterday the Duchess, who is a leading campaigner for the hospice movement, said: "I have opened quite a few hospices but never before have I had such a reception. It was amazing."

The welcome included flowers, a guard of honour of flag-waving children massed on the grassy banks leading up to the hospice, a parade of majorettes and music from the Basildon police band.

HEADLINERS: The Duchess, right, and Trudy Cox read about the opening in a later edition of yesterday's Echo

VIPs pay tribute to St Luke's Hospice

GREETINGS...for the Duchess of Norfolk, from the many schoolchildren who turned out to see her

In front of the hospice, a choir drawn from 15 local schools and Basildon Choral Society, sang while the Basildon Youth Orchestra played a special arrangement of a patriotic tune. The programme got well behind as she stopped to chat to children and thank conductors.

At the ceremony inside, unveiling the plaque in the long lounge used for the day patients, the Duchess said day centres contributed something very special to hospices.

"They are the first introduction of the patient and his family to the whole spirit of hospice care.

"In all sorts of ways they will make him or her feel much better and many of the family's anxieties will be lifted, and their confidence.

"The backing of a day centre ensures the patient can live at home. This is more and more the practice.

"I thank you for setting up another wonderful centre in this part of the country."

Tribute

She also mentioned how lovely it was for hospice pioneer, Matron Trudy Cox, that her parents could be here on the great day.

Pastor Frederick Muller and his wife, who are both over 90, had come from Germany for the occasion.

MP David Amess said thousands of people in the three districts of Thurrock, Billericay and Basildon had contributed to the magnificent achievement.

But though the inspiration had been Trudy's it would not have been possible without the tremendous support of husband Les, their three sons and her family.

He paid tribute to the Duchess's national Help the Hospices organisation which she founded, and said it raised £500,000 annually.

Basildon Council chairman Dave Marks said: "This is a great turn-out to see what Trudy has done with faith, hope, and a great deal of your charity.

Ideal

"Fobbing Farm could have been an office block. It is thanks to Trudy that it isn't. She got it only two weeks before that could have happened."

Mrs Joan Martin, chairman of Basildon and Thurrock Health Authority, said the hospice was in the ideal place. Being just across the road from the hospital it meant the health authority could put in nursing and other support staff more easily.

She said: "She was one of our district nurses with a dream. I am glad that dream has come true."

The tribute of Thurrock Mayor Coun Ken Evans was: "The human race throws out people who have this tremendous single mindedness and dedication.

"Some become Prime Ministers, some millionaires, others super sportsmen and women. Some of them turn out to be the Trudy Cox's of this world."

The Duchess stayed for more than five hours, touring round, meeting patients and helpers, talking to everyone, then going round the fete in the afternoon to talk to stallholders.

Debt

Les Cox said afterwards: "She was a lovely approachable lady. She really put herself out for us.

"In her conversation with us she said what a pity it was that all hospices had to struggle for money and she promised Help the Hospices would continue to lobby the Government for more help."

Trudy's family present included her sister-in-law from Nepal where Trudy's brother works as a civil engineer. Their church has given about £5,000 in support over the years to the Basildon hospice.

Les said that they still had a £136,000 loan debt to clear and although £830,000 had been raised over seven and a half years their expenditure had been £860,000.

Their newest venture is to be a second shop in Liberty Hall, near Basildon post office.

Visit Of Princess Diana

After the visit of the Duchess of Norfolk to open our new Day Care Unit more excitement was to come.

Just over six weeks had passed since Her Grace was with us and we were now getting ready for another royal welcome - Princess Di.

Once again we were all very excited and felt very honoured to be chosen for a visit from the Princess.

Our volunteer domestics were soon in full swing cleaning and polishing, inside and out, to make everything ready to welcome another royal guest.

Bill was in charge of raising the Union Jack on the hospice flag pole -('make sure it's the right way up, Bill !')

We again met with the police and Council members to plan and prepare for the great event.

Ken Sharp and Geoff Williams, our "Official Stewards" when the Duchess came, agreed to take on the role again for the Princess to make sure everything ran smoothly once more.

The day before the arrival of Her Royal Highness the area around the hospice was sealed off.

Our temporary flat upstairs in the old farmhouse was checked with sniffer dogs. The dogs also checked the new hospice extension.

Of course, they didn't find anything but it was a bit scary all the same watching them check everywhere including our personal items.

I like dogs but we were told we were not allowed to stroke the police dogs until they had completed their duties !

Downstairs, dustbins were turned upside down and cupboards were sealed.

Our family and friends needed special passes to visit us.

MB Marquees, who were so generous to us at the time of the Duchess of Norfolk visit, again helped us for Princess Di.

The night before the big day the most luxurious marquee arrived at St. Luke's, with all the silk lining and trimmings, flooring, chairs and anything else we required to make HRH's visit special.

Our thanks go once more to MB Marquees for their kindness to us in supplying all their equipment and the marquee free of charge.

Visit Of Princess Diana

Just before the moment arrived to welcome the Princess I quickly went upstairs to get ready.

My sister, Irmgard, found it hilarious and couldn't quite believe I hadn't arranged to spend the morning at the hairdressers getting an expensive hair-do.

Hence the photo opposite of me getting ready to meet a Princess !

I felt I could manage it quite easily myself, and hey presto, ten minutes later I was ready with the VIP's to welcome her.

In the unit our Day Care patients waited with great excitement. Well, to be honest, we were all very excited.

Our security police were in touch with their colleagues awaiting the arrival of the helicopter which was to land in Gloucester Park in the centre of Basildon.

They informed us it had landed and the Princess was ready to be driven to the hospice.

Just before that telephone call I went downstairs and Ken gave us his last minute instructions. Ken also found time to make sure the unveiling cord for the plaque was working properly as the Princess walked to the waiting car from the helicopter.

The Princess arrived, escorted by the Lord Lieutenant of Essex and met our little reception committee.

The Mayor of Thurrock, Chairman of Basildon Council and our MP David Amess with his wife Julia, Les and myself lined up ready for the big moment to greet Princess Di.

Visit Of Princess Diana

*Elsie makes the final adjustments to
one of her flower displays*

It was a very proud moment for me as I walked with the Princess towards the hospice doors and into the hospice reception.

Here we were greeted by Barbara and Lee, our volunteers who staffed the reception desk.

During the coffee break I was able to tell the Princess about the vision of a home for cancer patients.

I shared with her the needs of our patients and she just couldn't believe that all we had to begin our venture was just 25p

She was so interested in all our small beginnings and how it then developed.

It was time to receive her bouquet of flowers and for the official unveiling of the plaque recording her visit to St. Luke's.

The Princess meets our receptionist

Our first stop was the dining room, where Kathy, our housekeeper, had prepared a welcome cup of coffee. (We had been instructed by officials from Buckingham Palace that no other refreshments were to be served or required.)

The Princess unveils the plaque

Visit Of Princess Diana

The Princess also kindly signed a large coloured photograph of herself (it now hangs in our In Patient Unit close to the plaque), and our Hospice Guest Book.

Just before the unveiling of the plaque, Jean and Michael Rawlinson sang the beautiful duet - "If I Can Help Somebody"

It was lovely to see her listening to their different stories and showing genuine concern and love for them all. Day Care Dr. Jean and Management Chairman Gerry look on.

One of the first patients the Princess met was Minnie, the dear lady who gave us our first 25p donation to start us fundraising for St. Luke's.

Princess Diana was soon chatting to everyone as if she had known them for years instead of just meeting them for the first time.

Her concern for our patients and their problems was so genuine. Her easy manner and friendliness made everyone feel at home.

Then came the big moment the patients had been patiently waiting for as the Princess walked around the hospice, stopping and talking and joining in a scrabble game with our patients.

Visit Of Princess Diana

Ruth, Fundraising Co-ordinator for Basildon and Langdon Hills and a Management Team member escorted the Princess to the marquee and introduced her to our Fundraising Friends.

They had waited a long time for this moment but it was all worth it when the Princess arrived among them.

Meanwhile in the other parts of our crowded hospice guests waited patiently for the Princess to appear.

There was also a very packed Marquee outside with many more people all eagerly awaiting the Princess.

Surveying it all, with security uppermost in their minds, were the Lord Lieutenant of Essex with the Royal Escort.

Soon it was time for the Princess to move out of the hospice and into our marquee to meet our fundraisers.

The wonderful people who over many years gave their time, talents and financial gifts to help establish this special place.

We, St. Luke's, are still blessed with a committed community who continue to support and fundraise for us. It is only with their help we are able to continue with the care of our patients and their families.

Visit Of Princess Diana

All too soon our memorable day was fast coming to an end.

Princess Diana had literally been everywhere in the hospice, spoken, it seemed, to everyone and had made friends with everyone she had met.

As she stepped outside she was beseiged by the schoolchildren and the Princess didn't let them down.

She again took time to try to speak and shake hands with all of them. An impossible task for her but the children were delighted just to see her.

The Princess then left to drive back down to Gloucester Park and take her helicopter flight on to her next appointment in Essex.

Les and I thanked the Princess for her visit and everyone gathered outside to wave goodbye and to wish her a safe journey home.

Visit Of Princess Diana

Once back inside the hospice my initial reaction was one of extreme elation - (see photo opposite) - and unbridled joy at the success of the visit and felt that all we had hoped for in the visit had been achieved.

We had had a truly memorable day and all thanks to the wonderful Princess Diana.

It didn't take long before the first editions of our local paper, The Evening Echo had been delivered and we were all eagerly reading about what had happened to us on that day.

Our patients were more than ready for their lunch under the watchful eye of Jenni and Viv.

We had great fun reading, chatting, making sure all the facts were correct and re-living the royal visit with all its excitement.

Our special memories of Princess Diana's visit would remain with us for a very long time to come.

Visit Of Princess Diana

An official interview followed with Louise, the religious correspondent of the Evening Echo.

A warm farewell and thank you to our official security people.

And we were ready to start our own celebrations of the day with a good old fashioned 'knees up' helped by Bill Crafer and his accordion getting us in the mood.

'My Boy Bill' gets the sing-a-long going.

Hilda and Connie show off the official celebration cake we had for the occasion while with Maud's help our three volunteer cooks keep the cakes coming from the kitchen.

Visit Of Princess Diana

The large photo Princess Diana had signed during her visit brought out many admirers wanting to see it.

It is a beautiful photograph of a very beautiful and gracious lady.

The photograph hangs in the hospice today - Malcolm ('son No. 4') and Kathy had it framed for us as a gift. It is a permanent reminder of the day the Princess came to St. Luke's.

It looks as if my two grand-daughters Danielle and Nicola couldn't wait to put down on paper all that they had seen on this memorable day. They were with us all through that day.

Security supremo takes a well earned rest from his 'policing' duties.

My thanks to Geoff and to Ken for all their help, not only during the Princess visit, but also during the visit of the Duchess of Norfolk.

To this day Geoff is still supporting St. Luke's as member of the Basildon Choral Society.

My friends from the German Lutheran church in England celebrated the visit of Princess Di with me. My former patient Minnie from my District Nursing days checks out the hospice Information Display boards.

A big thank you to Roy Smith, our official hospice photographer. Many of the photos in these pages are examples of Roy's work.

Visit Of Princess Diana

At the end of a very special day Les and I relax for a special meal with our family. We still can't quite believe that we actually met such a famous member of the royal family.

Unbeknown to me - Christopher had sent a letter to Princess Di asking her to visit us a few years ago, so his wish finally came true.

PRINCESS Diana flew into Basildon today and fixed it at last for Christopher Cox.

Chris was only 13 when he first wrote and asked the Princess of Wales to help his mum's cause.

Mum is Sister Trudy Cox, matron of Basildon's St Luke's Hospice, and this morning her Royal Highness was able to do as Chris asked. She flew in by helicopter to see the hospice for herself.

The red RAF Wessex helicopter of the Queens Flight dropped from a brilliant blue sky into a curiously deserted Gloucester Park in Cranes Farm Road at 10am.

Only a handful of Royal watchers had gathered as the Princess was greeted by Lord Lieutenant Admiral Sir Andrew Lewis and Basildon police Superintendent Ken Smith.

Wearing a short, black pleated skirt and military style purple jacket with shiny brass buttons she walked briskly across the grass to a waiting Ford Granada Scorpio for the short drive to St Luke's.

An excited Chris, now 18, said this morning: "I couldn't believe it when mum heard she was coming at last.

"I remember thinking when I was 13 that it would be such a reward for mum and all the volunteers who were working so hard.

"I was very disappointed that she couldn't come then. But as I grew older I realised the hard work doesn't stop with a hospice."

Visit Of Princess Diana

This was how the local papers reported the visit of Princess Diana.

The reports convey exactly what a memorable day it was, not only for me but for our patients and their families and all our supporters.

ST LUKE'S HOSPICE GETS A SECOND ROYAL VISIT

Princess Di flies in with smiles and hope for hospice

by Louise Dray

PRINCESS Diana flew into Basildon on Tuesday and fixed it at last for Christopher Cox.

Chris was only 13 when he first wrote and asked the Princess of Wales to help his mum's cause.

Mum is Sister Trudy Cox, matron of Basildon's St Luke's Hospice, and last week her Royal Highness was able to oblige. She flew in by helicopter to see the hospice for herself.

The red RAF Wessex helicopter of the Queens Flight dropped from a brilliant blue sky into a curiously deserted Gloucester Park in Cranes Farm Road at 10am.

Only a handful of Royal watchers had gathered as the Princess was greeted by Lord Lieutenant Admiral Sir Andrew Lewis and Basildon police Superintendent Ken Smith.

Wearing a short, black pleated skirt and military style purple jacket with shiny brass buttons she walked briskly across the grass to a waiting Ford Granada Scorpio for the short drive to St. Luke's.

An excited Chris, now 18, said: "I couldn't believe it when mum heard she was coming at last.

Reward

"I remember thinking when I was 13 that it would be such a reward for mum and all the volunteers who were working so hard.

"I was very disappointed that she couldn't come then. But as I grew older I realised the hard work doesn't stop with a hospice."

In fact there were to be another five years of struggle before the hospice was built and furnished.

It's still not completely equipped and will have to finally top £1m before it can open.

So far £830,000 has been raised but £860,000 has been spent and there is a £136,000 debt to clear. Organisers need several months' running costs in hand before they open.

Target

So the original target of £400,000 in 1985 has trebled over the years. That seemed impossible enough in the beginning when their first donation in 1983 was 25p.

Building work began in January last year.

Sunshine visit to warm our hearts

THE world's favourite sugar-plum fairy princess provided the icing on the cake for patients, staff, fund-raisers and helpers during yesterday's visit to Basildon's triumphant St Luke's Hospice.

Matron Trudy Cox could hardly find enough words to describe the euphoria which Princess Diana had created during her hour-long visit.

She said: "It was absolutely terrific, wonderful, enjoyable — an honour and a privilege to have her here — most rewarding. It was the icing on the cake. Every minute of her visit was so good."

Trudy confided her initial nervousness to the Royal visitor, who soon put her at ease.

Trudy said: "She stayed an hour but I think she would have liked to stay longer. She could not get over the fact we have had so many helpers and supporters."

Many of them are now far-flung. But Trudy is determined that copies of the special day's Echo will be sent to Nepal, Switzerland, Africa and her native Germany.

Princess at hospice

PRINCESS Di dropped in on St Luke's Hospice on Tuesday — and brought happiness to crowds of well-wishers and fund-raisers who have made the dream a reality.

One of them was Mrs Minnie Bannister who was 72 yesterday (Thursday) and who gave the first donation of 25p in 1983 when the fund started.

She said: "I think its absolutely fantastic that has become of that five bob."

Minnie, who is paralysed, was taken in her wheelchair from Orsett Hospital for the great day wearing a borrowed shawl and pearls.

She said: "I was on a cloud when I met her. I don't remember what I said."

Visit Of Princess Diana

How the papers reported the visit of Princess Di

Princess drops in to see hospice

By LOUISE DRAY

PRINCESS Diana flew into Basildon today and fixed it at last for Christopher Cox.

Chris was only 13 when he first wrote and asked the Princess of Wales to help his mum's cause.

Mum is Sister Trudy Cox, matron of Basildon's St Luke's Hospice, and this morning her Royal Highness was able to do as Chris asked. She flew in by helicopter to see the hospice for herself.

The red RAF Wessex helicopter of the Queens Flight dropped from a brilliant blue sky into a curiously deserted Gloucester Park in Cranes Farm Road at 10am.

Only a handful of Royal watchers had gathered as the Princess was greeted by Lord Lieutenant Admiral Sir Andrew Lewis and Basildon police Superintendent Ken Smith.

Wearing a short, black pleated skirt and military style purple jacket with shiny brass buttons she walked briskly across the grass to a waiting Ford Granada Scorpio for the short drive to St Luke's.

From Page 1

An excited Chris, now 18, said this morning: "I couldn't believe it when mum heard she was coming at last.

"I remember thinking when I was 13 that it would be such a reward for mum and all the volunteers who were working so hard.

"I was very disappointed that she couldn't come then. But as I grew older I realised the hard work doesn't stop with a hospice."

In fact there were to be another five years of struggle before the hospice was built and furnished.

It's still not completely equipped and will have to finally top the £1m before it can open.

So far £830,000 has been raised but £860,000 has been spent and there is a £136,000 debt to clear. Organisers need several months running costs in hand before they open.

So the original target of £400,000 in 1985 has trebled over the years. That seemed impossible enough in the beginning when their first donation in 1983 was 25p.

Building work began in January last year and the first day patients were able to come in June this year.

A successful visit by the Duchess of Norfolk, chairman and founder Help the Hospices Movement, marked the opening of the day centre last month and two days later they heard about the Princess of Wales coming. But the eight beds for in patients can't be used until next summer when they have cleared debts and have the running costs.

Of course, it does not take long for reality to kick in again, does it ?

When we woke up the next morning it was business as usual at St. Luke's.

The jumble had started to arrive again. It would needed sorting, pricing and getting ready to be sent out to our various jumble sales to raise funds for the hospice.

Back down to earth again after our Royal visit - more jumble has arrived to be sorted !

Visit Of Princess Diana

The following day a letter arrived from Buckingham Palace with a thank you message from Princess Diana. It was with some pride we all read the letter. We had tried very hard to make the day a special one, not only for us, but for our royal visitor, too. Reading the sentiments expressed in the letter we reckon we had succeeded. Job well done !

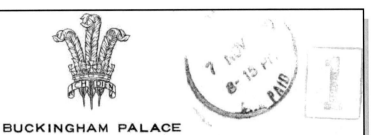

BUCKINGHAM PALACE

From: The Lady-in-Waiting to H.R.H. The Princess of Wales

7th November 1990

Dear Mrs Cox,

The Princess of Wales has asked me to thank you for all your help in making her visit to St. Luke's Hospice such a very interesting and memorable occasion.

Her Royal Highness was very pleased that she was able to open St. Luke's and was most impressed by all the facilities available and the delightful way in which it had been decorated. The Centre will clearly be a great asset to the community. The Princess much enjoyed meeting the patients, their families and members of staff as well as others connected with the Hospice and was most touched by her warm welcome.

Her Royal Highness has asked me to thank you also for the picture of St. Luke's which was kindly presented to her. It will be a marvellous memento of her visit.

I would also be grateful if you would kindly pass on Her Royal Highness's special thanks to Councillor Marks and of course Mr Cox for all their help in making the visit such a very rewarding and successful occasion.

Yours sincerely,

Laura Lonsdale

Mrs James Lonsdale

Our Garden at St. Luke's

The vision of the hospice was to create a homely atmosphere, not to replace home but to make it as home-like as possible. That homely feeling included having a garden to enjoy.

Many of you, I am sure, have walked around the St. Luke's gardens at some time. I know our patients and their families do. From the hospice bedroom's there is a beautiful view and many of our patients enjoy sitting with their families and loved ones on our patio.

Our garden is not just for show, though. It has many other uses. Fetes, special events and hospice services are held there. Day Hospice regularly holds parties and functions for our patients to enjoy.

The original farmhouse stood in approximately 3/4 acre of land. The building was first rented at a peppercorn rent and then later acquired from the Basildon Corporation Planning Department.

There were further strips of land at the rear of the Hospice towards Basildon Hospital and at the side of the lane leading up to the front of the hospice and Basildon College.

Once again I approached the Corporation, (this time their Estates Department) in order to add both areas of land for hospice gardens and extra car parking.

How great the news was when they agreed.

The front garden at the hospice

The rear garden at the hospice

Thank you God and thank you Basildon Corporation.

Looking back at the photographs at that time I am amazed at the transformation that has taken place. It was changed by a lot of hard work by a lot of people.

But first I would like to give you a potted history of how it all happened.

The 'hospice home' building was complete with its own front and back garden.

But now we needed a project manager. Someone who could organise a team of volunteer workers to transform the waste area into a garden.

I prayed to God to help us and guide that special person to us.

At that time the Rotaract members in Basildon (these were younger Rotarians) had fundraised a sum of money to help St. Luke's.

They approached Basildon Concord Rotary Club to seek advice how they should do this. It was then that I met Derek Adams. Derek was a Rotarian and the President of Basildon Concord Rotary for that year.

On meeting Derek I soon found out that Derek had been a project manager with the Ford Company at their tractor plant in Basildon.

Just what I was looking for !

Derek galvanised the Rotaract young men into a team of gardeners and work

Handing the spade over to Derek

started on clearing the front of the hospice to make room for gardens as well as for car parking space.

Derek was joined by his wife, Jean, and together they began tackling the giant sized weeds that had sprung up around the hospice. Another Concord Rotarian, Dennis, offered to help too.

The two 'D's and the 'J' worked as a great team.

They put in endless hours working in the hospice grounds. In a short while others joined and a regular working team was in force.

Our Garden at St. Luke's

Billericay Lions help clear the weeds

One of the first jobs the gardening team had to do was the mammoth task of clearing the weeds. Fortunately the Billericay Lions came to the rescue.

Derek and Jean get digging and weeding

Not a weed to be seen in Dennis's patch

Jean tackles the weeds

At the front of the hospice I wanted to put a children's play area. But first the weeds had to go. Once completed the play area was a success, not only because all children love swings and slides. I found it was somewhere where the little ones would open up to you. To tell you their feelings about mummy or daddy, or grandma or grandad who at that moment was in the hospice.

Swings and weeds don't mix

The completed children's play area

Once the weeds had all been cleared and the lawn seeded, we now needed a path to allow our patients and their families to walk around the garden or be pushed in a wheelchair.

A job for the two D's - Derek and Dennis !

Our Garden at St. Luke's

Derek and Dennis, the two D's, get cementing a path

This is where the path will be going. All the way round the outside of the lawn

Derek and Dennis start at the very beginning....

A little bit of shuttering here....

... a little bit more sand there ...

... and a little bit more cement here ...

...and there you have it - easy isn't it?

Our Garden at St. Luke's

The front area and the rear patio at the back of the hospice were beginning to take shape.

The next task was a seating area for the patients. It had to serve as a wind break, too.

Again Derek had just the right answer. A circular brick wall. Billericay Lions Club came back to help dig the foundations and, for bricklaying, Derek asked trainee students from a commercial firm to build the wall.

The Billericay Lions dig the foundations

The trainee brickies line up for a photo

The finished wall. Doesn't it look nice

A patient relaxing in the seating area

Our patients and their families love to come out to sit in this area and on the warmer days we have even pushed the patient's bed outside, too.

As you walk around the established and well looked after flower beds and other features please give thanks to God for his beautiful flowers and plants and for bringing to St. Luke's the right person and the right help at the right time.

We also thank God for encouraging others over the years to pick up the spade and the fork to continue maintaining the gardens and making them a haven for our patients and their families.

Our garden at St. Luke's is for our patients and their families to enjoy and relax in. That doesn't mean to say that a little help when offered is refused. Our gardeners always welcome a helping hand especially from patients.

Watering the easy way

Our Garden at St. Luke's

Sadly Dennis died before the gardens were fully established. We miss him dearly. Derek Adams retired from managing the garden project in 2007. They and the team of gardeners they had gathered around them are to be congratulated on their gardening achievements.

Before Derek retired there were a couple of award ceremonies to be performed.

I had the privilege of presenting Derek with his ten year as a volunteer certificate.

Derek and Jean receiving their ten year awards from 'headmistress' Trudy.

Derek was also honoured by Rotary International by being presented with an award by the President of Rotary International.

Derek explaining to the Rotary International President how the garden was created.

The Rotary International award was in recognition of Derek's and Dennis's work in creating St. Luke's garden.

The rear garden looking towards Basildon Hospital

Another view of the rear garden

The hospice patio

Our Garden at St. Luke's

I will leave this part of the book with a set of photographs which I hope will whet your appetite to come to our Summer Fete and see our gardens.

Derek's first gardening team

Path leading to the front of the hospice

A nice seat in the garden

St. Luke's Day Hospice

Rose beds in front of the hospice

A full house in our garden on Fete Days

Dinner is served Victorian style for a Day Care party on the garden lawn

134

Our Chapel Window

For the chapel we wanted a special window and again we encouraged our local schools to join in a competition. Many entries arrived, in fact, so many that it was very difficult to choose one.

Tressel tables were erected all around our unit, with all the entries displayed and Les and I just couldn't decide - there were so many exceptional entries.

Just then the wife of a former patient of mine arrived and I asked her to help me choose one.

I had visited her and her late husband in their home and had the privilege to witness their renewal of their wedding vows. One of our local C.of.E Chaplains officiated at the ceremony, attended by their two sons and their wives. It was very moving.

She had experienced our support during her husband's illness and then chose our chapel window. - - A Glimmer Of Light -- her words "That's what you were for us !"

I now needed someone to make the window and I found a young lady in Wickford who had a studio in her back garden.

How excited I was when I saw some of her work and asked her if she would be willing to help us with our chapel window.

She willingly agreed and what's even more wonderful, she didn't charge us but donated it to the hospice.

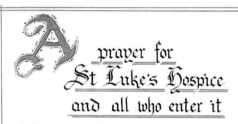

A prayer for St Luke's Hospice and all who enter it

Dear Lord Jesus,
We thank you for St Luke's Hospice. We pray for the work here of caring for our patients and their families. Guide us Lord, be with us so that those who are suffering sickness and pain, and those caring for them will be blessed and find your peace.
You promised to be with us always. Thank you for that promise.
Amen.

Day Care Open - Fundraising Continues

As our Day Care patients, staff and volunteers settled in, all other services continued as before: our Bereavement , Cancer Support, Sitting Services and Training of Volunteers.

You may remember that I mentioned before that we were fortunate to secure an interest free loan from the Health Authority but, of course, it still had to be paid back.

As a Management Committee we promised ourselves that that loan has to be re-paid in full before we would commence with our In-Patient care, so active fundraising continued.

Once our patients went home for the day, the Unit was, again, transformed by fundraising activities.

We held fashion shows

Talks and question and answer sessions were arranged.

We had Infomation diplays, handed out leaflets, gave talks. Groups of people would arrive and listened to our talks and encouraged to help us to raise more funds.

The young, and not so young, arrived helping and working hard.

We held jumble sales, especially the weekend sale.

Our volunteers were busy providing refreshments from our tea chalet as well as sorting through jumble and bric a brac.

We became real experts in the business of retail.

Our very first Fundraising Concert was in St. Margaret's Church, Stanford le Hope. Jean and Michael Rawlinson sang for the first time our traditional hospice duet - Bless This House: Concerts were held inside the hospice unit, too

Getting Ready For In Patients

As well as all the activities in and around the hospice our volunteers worked hard in our hospice shops - i.e. a unit in Liberty Hall in Basildon Town Centre and Peggy's famous jumble sales from home.

People opened their own homes for coffee mornings, bring and buy activities and garden parties, in short, throughout our catchment area an awful lot of people worked very hard, raising funds, giving practical and prayerful support.

Our thanks to everyone involved, including our 999 services, schools, churches, clubs.

The Lions, organising the Basildon carnival, donated their income to the Hospice.

Night Sister Sue

In short wherever people met or worked we were present giving talks and had information leaflets and displays, literature informing about the work of the hospice.

Reaching the end of our first year caring for our Day Care patients we had to start to prepare for

Day Care Staff Nurse Helen

interviewing and training of staff for our In Patient Unit, as well as increasing our staff in Day Care.

This enabled us to increase the number of patients attending.

Sue Greenham was appointed as Night Sister, Helen Room as Day Care Staff Nurse while Jenni Newton transferred from Day Care to Sister of the In Patient Unit.

Meanwhile four of us, Viv, Sue, Jenni and myself were busy preparing the Induction Course for our nursing staff. We also had meetings with our pharmacist to prepare for the delivery of medical supplies.

Colin Wind, a community pharmacist had for many years helped in the promotional work of the hospice. Colin was the Health Authority pharmacist and he met with us to discuss our future needs.

As with all nursing homes, we also had to meet with the Registration Team at regular intervals. They included representatives from the Health Authority, Health & Safety Executive and the fire and catering services.

Pharmacist Colin Wind with his two assistants

I became familiar with so many rules and regulations that my feeling of insecurity increased by the minute.

I had had no idea that there were so many directives, orders, rules and regulations to observe. It was frightening and very, very scary.

Our photo shows meetings with our pharmacists held in our flat at Fobbing Farm.

Our prayer chain worked overtime and it worked.

I attended courses, visited more establishments, had crash-lectures on personel and disciplinary management, gradually as I learned all the intricate details (the rules and regulations) of Nursing Home Management (the classified term used by the Registration and Inspection Team).

I became more assertive and confident. It was good to have the reassurance that Les was there as administrator who was excellent. More and more official files appeared in the office with everything we had to adhere to neatly marked ready to be inspected by any member of the Registration Team.

Our First Salaried Secretaries - Personal, Medical and Fundraising

I, in the meantime, now desperately needed a personal secretary. We advertised and had nearly 40 applications.

The person who was to become my personal secretary had to be someone who could cope with my many roles as Matron/Manager/Fundraiser and be familiar with employment and personel issues. In fact, a very special person.

First we held a general open meeting where all these dear people arrived, approx 40, hoping to be appointed. We shortlisted and then shortlisted again.

But I remember so clearly while they were all seated in the bay area of the Hospice one person who stood out, seated two seats from the left.

This applicant was shortlisted again and then not only interviewed by me, but also by a qualified secretary to check out for me her secretarial qualifications and experience.

My Personal Secretary Sue

In short, this young person who caught my eye in the very first meeting with the applicants had all the necessary qualifications needed for a 'perfect secretary'. Sue Hunt was duly appointed and from now on shared not only with me all the issues I tried to cope with but also was a great support and later a dear friend to me for the whole time as the Matron/Manager at the Hospice.

How she put up with me all those years I never know and both Sue and I could write another book titled 'being the first Secretary at St.Luke's.

Because my fundraising responsibilites were increasing at that time Sue, for a short time,became my secretary concentrating on all aspects of fundraising.

I also needed a secretary with medical qualifcations for the clinical part of my work. Dawn was appointed and I soon found out she had the same sense of fun as I did. When Dawn left to have a baby Di Burton joined.

Dawn and I having a 'midnight feast' - with Slimfast !!

New medical secretary Di with 'my Sue'

Allison Jones completed my trio of secretaries when she joined St. Luke's as my fundraising secretary.

Allison has now moved on to become part of our Fundraising team.

In fact all three secretaries are still with the hospice.

Fundraiser Allison

Sue is now secretary to the Head of Care; Di is secretary to Chief Executive; and Allison is in Fundraising

Appointment Of Medical Director

As mentioned in a previous chapter, Dr. Jean Maxwell, was a GP in the Basildon area. Dr. Jean was one of the Doctors I was responsible to while working as a District Nurse. She had been our Hon. Medical Director during the first year of Day Care.

Dr. Jean with her dog, Selva

We now needed a permanent Medical Director. Dr. Jean had been at St. Francis Hospice in the meantime getting more Hospice experience.

Dr. Anthony Smith was the Medical Director at St. Francis. He was a very experienced Hospice Doctor and Jean felt drawn to stay at St. Francis under the Directorship of Dr. Anthony Smith where she would gain a lot more experence.

We were sorry to lose Jean but thanked her for her love and commitment to St. Luke's. First, to me personally when times were tough as a District Nurse and I needed support and understanding. She then agreed to join the Management Committee at St. Luke's and worked many years as a member.

Once Day Care opened she became our Hon. Medical Doctor overseeing our first year of Day Patient care while continuing as a GP.

We know she will continue to remember us in her prayers and will remain a true friend and colleague to us here at St. Luke's. Thank you, Jean, for everything.

Incidentally, she even danced for the hospice Day Care party, as a member of the Scottish Dancing group.

Dr. Jean with her Scottish Dance grouup friends

This meant we now needed to advertise for a permanent Medical Director.

It needed to be a very special person, able to work in the hospice environment together with a team of Nurses, Social Workers and Chaplains, and, of course, our large team of volunteers whom the hospice relied on heavily.

In other words, a person who can adapt to all sorts of usual and unusual situations.

He or she needed to be up to date in the field of palliative care and all that entails to give the very best of care to relieve our patients of any distressing pain and symptoms they may experience. We nursing staff also needed guidance in the latest methods of palliative care and continued education and updating is vital to maintain the standard of care required. He/She, needed to be part of the teaching team for all staff and external health care workers.

As a Christian based hospice we were anxious to have a like-minded person who will be able to join us in our prayer times for our patients, their families, friends, the staff and all involved with the hospice. In short, a very special person.

Dr. Elizabeth Joins St. Luke's

How glad we were to be able to appoint Dr. Elizabeth Jones who lived in Eltham, South London, married to Paul with two little girls, Victoria and Rosemarie.

Dr. Elizabeth had trained as a G.P. before entering Palliative Care in 1986. She gained experience at St. Christopher's Hospice in Sydenham before working in the local community and hospitals of Greenwich.

Dr. Elizabeth Jones

Here she set up specialist palliative care services which have continued to develop over the years. Elizabeth was attracted to the role of Medical Director at St. Luke's because this offered the opportunity to further develop her own skills and those of other staff within a Christian environment.

Dr. Elizabeth's two children, Victoria and Rosemary

Elizabeth hoped to be able to sell her house and move nearer to St. Luke's. The Medical Director needed to be living within a radius of 10 miles to the hospice for on call and eventual emergency duties.

Elizabeth, a very caring person with experience in palliative care was duly appointed as Medical Director. Right from when we first met there was a good rapport between us.

It was so good and reassuring to have a permanent Medical Director. with whom we could now share the responsibilities of caring for our patients and their families.

Elizabeth was a great source of information and an extremely good teacher. We were very fortunate to have her as our Medical Director.

As well as having Dr. Elizabeth as our Medical Director and being responsible for any clinical decisions we also needed medical cover during her absence, such as holidays, night duty and weekends.

I visited Basildon Hospital, adjacent to St. Luke's, to seek out consultants who were willing to cover those times on a voluntary basis.

In other words, no financial reward, just the thanks of a very grateful staff at St. Luke's.

We were so grateful to Doctors Lee, Woodgate and Willoughby who voluntarily covered for Dr. Elizabeth.

Likewise our local GPs joined in the rota system. Doctors Ron Sharpe, Anthony Millwood and Chris Williams.

My heartful thanks to all those kind doctors who again gave of their time freely covering the medical needs of our patients and supporting the nursing staff during Dr. Elizabeth's off duty time.

Thank you all so much.

Interviewing and choosing Nursing Staff

It was now essential to advertise for Nursing Staff and approximately 120 nurses applied.

Looking through the application forms we shortlisted for the first time and informal interviews commenced.

We not only needed caring and committed staff but they also obviously needed to have the required qualifications and experience with the right personality.

In those days hospices were few and far between so many applicants had not actually worked in a hospice before.

It was also necessary for the appointees to be willing to undergo a three week induction course as well as continuous training and updating.

Personally, I also felt it necessary to have a range of ages to identify with our young patients (for the first two years we also admitted children until Little Haven Childrens Hospice opened), as well as more mature ones.

Our photo shows Jenni, myself and Viv practising our interviewing techniques on Barbara, a Hospice volunteer.

Once we had decided on an applicant my final consideration would always be "would I like to be nursed by this person if I was totally dependent".

The interviews were quite extensive. I was so grateful to the Personnel Department at Basildon Hospital as well as the police who shared with me interviewing techniques during a few crash courses during my personal preparation as Matron of St. Luke's.

Gradually I began to feel more confident. Viv, Jenni and I carefully chose the questions that needed to be asked. Between us we decided who would ask which question. This gave us the opportunity to observe.

Obviously, we tried hard to make the interviewees feel confortable and at ease but at the same time it was so important to have the right person.

We prayed before the interviews, asking God for help, guidance and wisdom.

At the end of the interviews we were blessed with a wonderful team of nurses, who gelled together and gave their very best.

Some of the original nurses are with us to this day. Some after a few years left to widen their experience in other areas of nursing.

Many joined us years later again as Bank Nurses. Their commitment to the hospice never left them.

Induction Course

Prior to the commencment of our nursing staff we worked hard to prepare for a Three Week Induction Course.

We urgently needed teaching material, such as overhead projector, slide shows, TV and Video Recorders, Flip Chart stand, Acetates and other teaching material.

There was very little money available at the time so the members of the Management Committee offered to help us in practical ways.

One offered a TV set, someone else a video recorder.

There were more items outstanding at the end of our meeting so I asked for money to buy the following missing items.

* Overhead projector and stand;
* Flip Chart & Stand
* Acetates, pens, paper etc.

The money was approved. It was understood that I would spend as little money as possible.

The meeting ended at 22.30 hours. I went in my office where I found a scrap of paper with a note to say that a couple, Bob and Gill, had visited us while we were at the meeting and without knowing our need, offered to donate the missing items.

God's hand was at work once again; all we had to do is trust him.

Together we thanked God for leading Bob and Gill to the hospice at that moment.

Some time later I gave a talk to the Basildon Inner Wheel Ladies about St. Luke's history and plans for the future.

I told them about our needs and shared with them the miracle of the way we had received some of our teaching items and the items on loan from the Management Committee.

A short time after this we had a visit from the Inner Wheel.

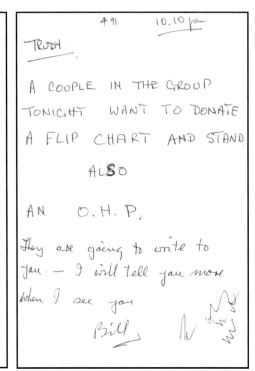

The gifts presented to the hospice

Our sincere thanks to the Basildon Inner Wheel Ladies

Following my talk they had raised enough money to provide St. Luke's with a slide projector, TV and Video Recorder and the stands needed for them.

The Three Week Induction Course

The context of the Induction Course was based on 'Palliative Care.'

In other words, "Hospice Philosophy" - seeing the whole patient with all his/her needs as well as that of the family.

Some of the Subjects covered:-

* Pain & Symptom Control
* Emotional needs.
* Spiritual Needs.
* Social Needs and Concerns.
* Practical & Financial Needs.
* Communications, i.e., breaking bad news.
* Support for the patients and family during
* The illness.
* Bereavement Support.

We were very fortunate to have accomplished speakers who gave freely of their time and expertise.

Consultants/Medical Directors/Doctors from neighbouring Hospices were our speakers who covered all aspects of Hospice Care.

Dr. Colin Trask - Southend Hospital.

Dr. David Frampton - Farleigh Hospice, Chelmsford.

Dr. Mark Stuart - Fairhaven Hospice, Southend.

Dr. Ann Naylor, Basildon Hospital.

Dr. Elizabeth Hall, St. Helena Hospice, Colchester.

Dr. Jean Maxwell, St. Francis Hospice, Havering.

Other speakers were:-

Pat Frisby, Sue Smee, Lelie Holmes, Jo West, Jenny Salkeid, Rosemary Frampton, Alan Herber, Chris Powney, Mr Green, Jill Buckland, Romy Bacon, Lorraine Cosgrove, John Rogers. Also Jane McLaughlin and Jackie McPherson, MacMillan Nurses.

Thank you all so much. No way would we have been able to pay for your valuable service.

It would have been much too costly. You saved the hospice thousands of pounds

Dr Elizabeth, Sisters Sue -Viv - Jenni - and myself, and our Hospice Chaplain, Rev. Derek Tuck, were part of the Teaching Team.

We were also fortunate to have representatives from Napp Laboratories and Parker Nursing Aids.

Dame Cecily Saunders, Founder of the Modern Hospice Movement put it like this:

You matter to the last moment of life. We will do all we can not only to help you to die peacefully but to live until you die.

A little verse I have reproduced here.

> Ideal
>
> Free of pain
> Alert in mind
> At peace with family and friends
> Minimum of un-finished business
> Confident in faith and at peace with God

Education and updating is important in any profession but, in the clinical area, we are concerened with change is so fast that it's often difficult to keep up.

We have a high standard to adhere to. This was maintained through regular study days/attending courses, continuous updating and learning. St. Luke's continues to this day to be a home of excellent care.

Equipment is improved continuously and our nurses attend practical sessions like lifting and handling and first aid etc.

The list goes on and on - taking in as well all the necessary Government requirements.

A registration team visits regularly, comprising a Health & Safety Officer - Pharmacist - Medical Officer - Catering and Domestic representatives.

The responsibility of this team is to make sure that all the Rules and Regulations are adhered to.

Viv, Sue, Jenni and I worked hard to make the course as comprehensive as possible but also fun.

There was lots of laughter heard around the hospice. I have always found that as a nurse you also need to have a sense of humour.

After all, laughter and tears are very much related, they seem to go together very well.

Our Nursery

As some of our staff were young with small children I asked Social Services and Basildon Council for permission to have a nursery at the Hospice during that time.

We had a qualified Nursery Nurse with two helpers in attendance.

The young mums were able to share their mealtimes with their children -- as well as some playtime.

It was so nice seeing mums and children together.

We were always anxious to have a family atmosphere at the hospice.

This was the start of it and to this day it's the same - a real family feeling around this lovely place.

Induction Course Caterers

Throughout the whole three weeks our valuable kitchen staff led by our own Cook-Housekeeper Kathy did us proud once again.

Generous buffet meals, coffee and tea times were

provided for us all in the true Hospice-Kathy way, so much so, I think we all put on a few pounds here and there.

P.S. I would like to point out, in case the reader thinks we were wasting Hospice money on meals, most of the food was donated to the hospice, therefore it is at very little cost to St. Luke's.

Housekeeper Kathy

Kathy's volunteer caterers - l to r: Connie, Hilda, Maud

We, as hospice staff and volunteers have to pay for our meals.

Thank you, always, to the generous local major store who helped us in this way then, and still does today.

Following the Induction Course and the receiving of Certificates of Attendance by our new nurses we all went out for a Celebration Meal.

End Of Induction Course Celebration

A selection of photos from my albums to give you a flavour of our Study Days

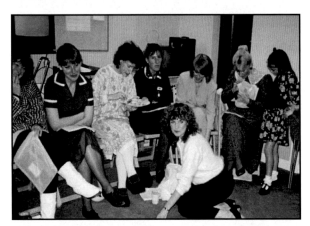

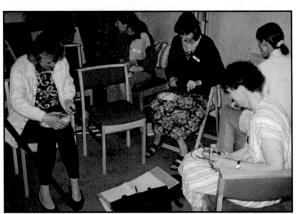

Official Photographs

Following staff interviews, induction course and the celebration meal we all posed for the first official photographs. The first photo is taken of our staff in the In Patient Unit. On that day the Chairman of Basildon Council, Cllr. Dave Marks is seated next to me, with Dr. Elizabeth on the right and Les, Administrator on the left.

For our second photograph we all went outside and posed again for the camera in front of the In Patient Unit of the Hospice. This time we were joined by members of the Management Committee and hospice volunteers.

We are now ready to receive our first In Patient.

Our First In Patient Arrives

My personal secretary, Sue, our nursing staff, our Medical Director all settled in and having completed the Induction Course, we were now ready to welcome our first In-Patient.

The date: 11th June 1991 - exactly one year and six days after our first day Care patient arrived, almost to the day of our first anniversary.

We had celebrated our Anniversary Service with thanksgiving in our hearts; grateful that our interest free loan from the Health Authority had been re-paid as we had promised to do.

Here we were - waiting for the ambulance to arrive bringing Dot, our patient, with her husband Jack. Suddenly, here they were.

Dot, as she preferred to be called, and Jack knew all about St. Luke's. At my home assessment visit prior to admission I shared with them what to expect as all patients, when they are first referred and then arrive, are obviously apprehensive and nervous.

Our first patient arrives

But Dot and Jack were such a dear couple and just grateful that soon Dot would feel much more comfortable.

She settled in well and was so grateful when we explained that Jack could stay at the Hospice with her, if that's what they both wanted.

After a nice cup of tea and a little rest following her journey Dot was ready to meet with the nursing staff and Dr. Elizabeth.

As mentioned before we are a patient led unit: the patient shares with us their needs and together the care plan is established.

Our Day Care patients shared one room, the In-Patients had single rooms, but everything else was shared by both - Day Care and In-Patients.

That worked really well and it was a pleasure to see the patients share their meals together and chatting with each other.

Gradually more and more patients were admitted. Referrals were via the GPs, the patient or the family, or via District or Mcmillan Nurses all with GP's knowledge.

A good relationship with all carers is vital, be it in the home, hospital or hospice.

Our kitchen staff once again did us proud. They go to each patient and explain what's on that day's menu. But should the patient have a special wish everyone tries their hardest to please. This kind of individual care continues to this day and makes St. Luke's the special place it is.

Husband, Jack, and family visiting Dot in her hospice room

Our First In-Patient Arrives

How the press reported our first admission to St. Luke's

First overnight patient for St Luke's Hospice

ST LUKE'S Hospice is fully operational at last. There will be a light burning 24 hours a day at St Luke's from now on because the first of the eight in-patients has been admitted.

At a cost of £1,100 a week per bed, terminally ill cancer patients will be cared for in the purpose-built hospice on the hill opposite Basildon Hospital.

Waiting at the door to greet her first in-patient Matron Trudy Cox could hardly believe the day had come after eight years' struggle.

The tears were near as she said: "I nearly gave up more than once."

But Trudy's cause was adopted by the town and an army of friends and helpers who kept it going, giving moral support to her and her family until the building was ready and equipped.

The crowning glory came with the visit of the Princess of Wales to congratulate them all last November.

The first patient to spend a night in the hospice, Mrs Doris Johnson, 76, of Gordon Road, Corringham, was carried in on a stretcher. She is terminally ill with cancer.

Husband Jack, 78, said: "This is a red letter day, my wife being the first patient to stay. I have had wonderful help from the hospice nurses in caring for her at home.

'This place is out of this world, they are so caring, they are really dedicated."

The Johnsons are great-grandparents and Mr Johnson has been bringing his wife to the hospice day centre until she could come in to be looked after.

But administrator Les Cox, Trudy's husband, warned that the hospice would cost £450,000 a year to run and they were as much dependent on the public for funds as ever.

He said: "Once the new building is up people tend to give a sigh of relief, sit back and say: 'That's that.'

"But, in common with most places like this, we are going to be hard-pressed. We just pray that we can keep up with the demand."

The hospice received an £80,000 share of the £8 million the Government distributed among about 150 hospices in Britain last year.

Les said: "This was a great relief and we hope we are going to get some more this year from the Government, but, of course, that's not certain."

But unlike many hospices it gets no cash help from local health authority

THE crispy clean sheets with hospital corners were on the bed in St Luke's Hospice when the first respite patient was admitted last week.

Matron Trudy Cox described the day as a memorable occasion as Doris Johnson from Corringham began her two week respite stay at the Basildon hospice which until now has only had day care patients.

Trudy said: "It was a very big occasion and a real day for us. Doris is staying in bedroom two for two weeks just to give her husband a break."

The hospice for the terminally ill will be admitting appropriate residential and respite patients over the next two weeks.

Polish-born Trudy said: "Doris is getting thoroughly spoiled, she is absolutely delightful and grateful for any little task. She reminds me so much of my own mother it makes me feel homesick."

Husband Jack Johnson said: "Doris has been going to the hospice for six months now and is very privileged to be accepted as the first in-patient.

"Although I love my wife dearly and care for her as best I can, I also need a break and some time to myself so I can be refreshed and ready for her return home.

"Doris is in the best possible hands and the love and nursing care given to her is unquestionable and I know that she also will enjoy her stay with her friends."

All patients at the hospice have full medical attention.

Daily Life with our Day Care & In-Patients Together

Once we had admitted our first patient, of course, demand for our services just grew and grew but so did the activities we provided to try to create a homely and welcoming atmosphere for our Day Care and In Patients.

We invited a lady harpist to entertain us and play a duet with one of our patients

 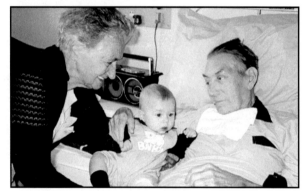

A lovely picture of a son playing to his father and a grandchild meeting his grandad.

One of our patients was a Salvationist and wanted to hear her colleagues play.

 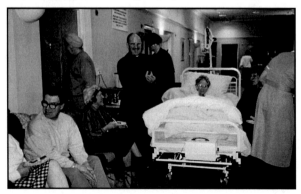

We invited dancers from the Royal Ballet to perform for our patients in the unit

At this time In-Patients and Day Care were together and shared the Unit area.

Daily Life with our Day Care & In-Patients Together

We've had a number of wedding ceremonies performed in the hospice, and services are a regular feature of hospice life. Of course, if the wedding happens to be of a staff member or volunteer our patients are never left out of the celebrations.

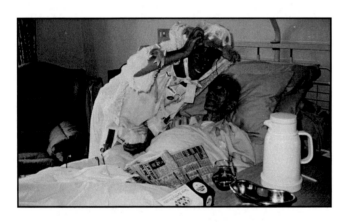

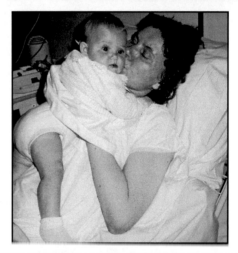

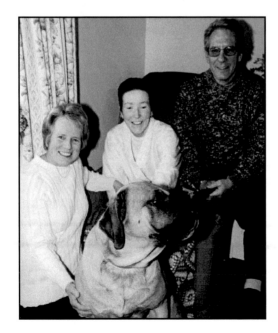

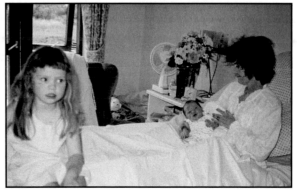

We have always encouraged children and grandchildren to be with us and their families and, of course, the family pet must not be left out either.

Daily Life with our Day Care & In-Patients Together

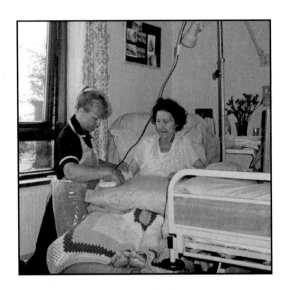

Lots of T.L.C. (tender loving care) and making life as normal as possible has always been the aim of St. Luke's, its staff and its volunteers.

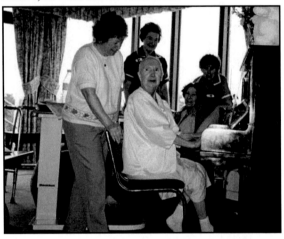

And, what could be better than a welcome cuppa served by Jill?

A full course meal courtesy of Matron Trudy and Trustee Chairman Gerry

Fully Operational

Now years later, looking through my photographic records, newspaper cuttings, Matron's Reports and general notes, it brought back to me so many memories.

Every photograph I looked at reminded me of those early moments, remembering our dear patients and their families, each of whom had their own story to tell.

It was also good to see our staff settling in and working so well together: Dr. Elizabeth, our nurses, our social workers, chaplains and our volunteers.

We had a great team and I remember being so proud of them.

Together we shared happy times, difficult times, and sad situations. Because we worked as a team, supporting one another when needed, we all felt very privileged to work in such a special place.

During meal times in our dining area, our In-patients if they were well enough, joined the Day Care patients, chatting with one another and even those patients with little appetite felt encouraged by their fellow patients.

Kathy with her catering team would make sure individual needs were met, such as special diets or dishes.

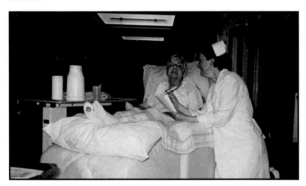

Our photograph shows just such a moment. Kathy, discussing the menu with one of our patients. I remember once a patient who had been quite poorly and had been eating very little really fancied jellied eels.

One of our volunteers drove all the way to Leigh on Sea to buy some eels. Although not many were eaten to see the patient's happy face was our reward.

Day and In-Patients Care continued as before with the patients appreciating the added care of different therapies we were able to provide, such as. physiotherapy, reflexology, and aromatherapy carried out by trained staff and volunteers in that field.

Clinical assessments addressing pain and any distressing symptoms were then and continued to be our first priority.

Patients enjoyed social activities, outings, meeting and sharing with each other.

Whenever I called in on my daily round, either in the In-Patient Unit or to meet with patients and their families in Day Care, it was so heart-warming to see their smiling faces.

We could fill another book with all the 'thank you's' received, not only from the patients but their families as well.

The following year life went on at the hospice in its usual way. We continued to hold Induction Courses and further training services for our new volunteers.

Thankfully people continued to arrive to help, giving freely of their time, skills and energy.

Our Bereavement Work - our Sitting Service and Cancer Support had now entered its 8th year. You may remember that I wrote in an earlier article about that valuable work.

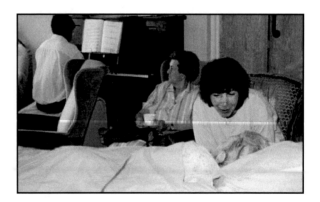

On Sunday afternoons we always hold a short service in the In-Patient Unit. The service is led by our own Hospice Chaplains and churches in our catchment area.

Fully Operational

These services continue to this day. We are grateful to all our local churches who were willing to spend Sunday afternoons with us sharing Jesus's love.

Any patient who wanted to attend these services joined us. We always made it clear that, although the hospice was a Christian based hospice, we respected all our patients needs.

Some wanted to attend and we used to take the bed into the Bay area for the patient to participate.

Some patients left their bedroom doors open to listen to the hymns, others maybe closed their doors.

The chaplains would always check with the nurses to see who among the patients had requested a visit.

Should patients want to see their own priest, chaplain or leader of their church we would contact them to visit the patient.

And, of course, all the time we continued giving talks to folk who invited us.

We use every opportunity to fundraise and encouraging other people to support us helping the hospice to enable us to continue to care for our dear patients and their families.

Every now and again schoolchildren or other musical entertainers would come and visit making for lovely moments of listening, followed by refreshments and happy chatter.

A beautiful picture of In Patient and Day Care together sharing a Christmas Nativity performance by the children of Swan Mead School

Another memorable photo was the visit of the string section of the Royal Opera Orchestra

My photos have their own captions but I would like to add that we tried to involve In-Patient and Day Care sharing together on many other occasions too.

It was so good to see our patients enjoying themselves and truly becoming members of our 'Hospice Family'

I thanked God many times fo rmaking the dream of a hospice in our area a reality.

Swan Mead schoolchildren talking to our patients

Our Chapel service with Peter and Shirley

St. Luke's Hit By Cash Crisis

Hospice pleads for help in wake of £97,000 loss

We are in debt !

We had now been fully operational for just over a year but were in real financial difficulties.

That hit me hard.

St. Luke's is a Community Hospice - supported by the community and serving the community, and now we needed help and understanding from our community.

The newspaper cuttings show our press release which we felt duty bound to publish.

The day of the press release I felt very upset and at one point I went to the farthest end of the Hospice garden, sobbing.

It had to come out and, when I do cry, I do it in style, my eyes were swollen, my face red. I just felt so very sad that it had happened.

Was it our fault ? Should we have concentrated more on fundraising ?

I went to the end of the garden because that was the only place where I could be alone, undisturbed, or so I thought.

Would you believe it. Someone only sent the local Evening Echo newspaper reporter to take a photograph of me and get a statement about the debt.

Well, of all the times to have your photo taken it had to be now.

He was most apologetic and waited a moment for me to sort myself out.

I am so grateful to God that he gave me a happy character. Yes, I am sensitive but mostly I can recover reasonably quickly and be positive again.

Cash crisis as hospice appeals to fundraisers

ST Luke's Hospice is struggling for survival and appealing to Thurrock folk to help it out of a desperate financial crisis.

pumping thousands a month int the hospice but it needs to step u by nearly £2,000 a wee

Trudy's praying for help to save town's hospice

finances report

A STATEMENT on the financial position of cash-starved St Luke's Hospice, Basildon, was due to be made today. But matron Trudy Cox stressed there was no danger the hospice, which last month celebrated one year of in-patient care, would close.

Each of the eight beds costs £60,000 a year. That works out at £1,154 a week, £165 a day or £6.88 an hour.

PRAYING

A £97,000 first-year deficit has cast a dark cloud over St Luke's Hospice in Basildon.

The dream ambition of matron Trudy Cox and her husband Les is causing them sleepless nights as they struggle to find ways to pull in more cash. But they are determined they will succeed.

Trudy said: "God's will we will continue. But we must be actively involved. We are praying for people's hearts to be moved into action."

Each of the eight beds costs £60,000 to run. Bereavement

God called us to do this work. God will help us through this crisis, of this I was sure.

Now, **He** just had to take over and take over **He** did.

Cash Crisis

Prayers were sent and answered and my confidence which had momentarily been lost, came flooding back. With God's help, our supporters, fundraisers, and our community, we beat the crisis, and were the stronger for it.

Every letter and note we received was with a gift, some small, some large, but all were given with love and support.

Our friends in our caring community had come up trumps once again.

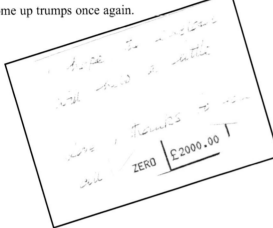

I've selected just a few of the messages and donations we received to show you how everyone helped and supported us.

I was so grateful and thankful that I lived among a community that was so very caring.

Please accept our sincere thanks fo[r] very kind donation of £5.00 which y[ou] kindly handed in at our Charity Sho[p] response to our appeal in the local[ ]

We were so encouraged by your gift know that you were concerned about needs.

On behalf of patients and staff ple[ase] our heartfelt thanks.

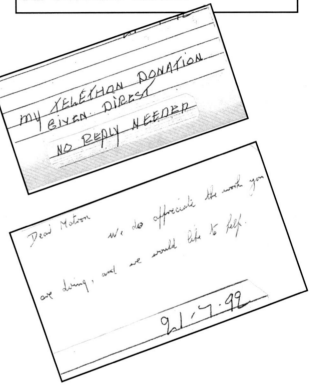

Dear Trudy and Les,

We enclose a cheque for £300-00 which might help towards your bread or milk bills??

Sorry to see the article in the paper saying you are running at a great loss but also feel that, having made people aware of your plight, they will do all they can to support you through this difficult time.

Perhaps you could send me a few of your forms for becoming friends of the Hospice and advise procedure for arranging Covenant.

We can understand how sad you must be feeling having now opened and doing so much good for the patients, but keep your spirits up as we are sure all those who are concerned about the future of St. Luke's will rally round.

Kind regards,

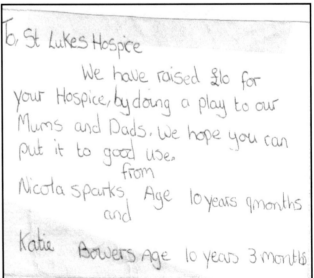

Solving The Debt Problem

'How Do You Solve A Problem Like a £97.000 Debt?'

Looking at my Matron's Report from August 1992 I see it was a case of all hands to the pump after we had published the debt press release in July of that year.

I had written that the telephone had not stopped ringing from members of the public offering support - financial and practical.

It was obvious our community had supported our decision to 'go public' about our financial problems and keep everyone informed and sharing with them the bad news as well as the good.

We took the decision to produce our own St. Luke's News as an aid to inform everyone what was happening and to encourage their support and help.

We made local radio appeals which generated more financial support. We stepped up the distribution of our Covenant and Friends of the Hospice forms. Again this helped as we received completed forms back.

We looked at our staffing and costs. I had contacted Fair Haven Hospice in Southend regarding their staffing levels and found they compared favourably with St. Luke's.

I was quite relieved to hear this as the planning of our Hospice, the staffing levels and other developments, were carried out following their advice, guidance and expertise.

We had also followed the actual requirements of staffing levels from the Registration Officer.

We tried to reduce our employment of 'Bank' nurses (outside agency help). We did have some success in this by covering annual leave and staff absence ourselves but always in our minds was the overiding aim of not reducing the amount of care given to our patients.

All these initiatives helped but we still had quite a way to go. Trying to solve a problem like a debt of £97,000 was proving very difficult.

It was obvious it needed something much, much bigger.

Something to capture the community's imagination and to get everyone involved and fired up wanting to help.

Busker Bill in action

At this stage I could almost start to write like a playwright.... 'Enter stage left - Bill Crafer'

Again and again God answered our prayers in times of great need.

A few years before our opening in 1990, Bill had learned about St. Luke's and our need for volunteers.

Bill is very much led by God and it shows in his daily life and his work as a volunteer at St. Luke's. Bill truly is Christianity in Action.

I first got to know Bill when he helped as a driver at our Bereavement Support meetings which were, in those early days, held at our house in Clay Hill Road, Basildon.

Bill is a very committed Christian. His love in action is evident in all he does, no matter what it is.

He is also a very gifted man. Someone who could fix almost anything and what's more is prepared to do it with a big smile.

There aren't many people living in our community who haven't heard of Bill.

'My boy Bill', as I affectionately called him, had been with us as a volunteer for approximately two years when the toll of continuous fundraising to establish a Hospice finally caught up with me. I became ill and was taken to hospital.

Following my discharge I was told I needed a lot of rest. Bill came to see me to see if he could help lighten my load.

Of course he could! I had prayed for someone with enthusiasm and love for the Hospice and faith in its establishment and God. My prayers had been answered.

Bill had a desk allocated to him in my office and this became his second home.

Solving The Debt Problem

At one time we used to tease Bill that we would make up a bed for him in the office so he could sleep there as well.

From this desk Bill helped me with many of my fundraising efforts and talks, speaking about the work of the hospice.

It was an on-going process of encouraging our community to support us.

It wasn't long before Bill was organising his own fundraising events and speaking on behalf of St. Luke's in churches, clubs and meeting people.

When our debt problem was announced and the public told about it, Bill immediately wanted to help, but how?

Bill did what he always does in these situations. He prayed, told Jesus and waited for the answer.

Soon Bill felt God had led him to think of a very special fundraising idea - the brilliant idea of the **HOSPICE-THON.**

A massive year-long fundraising extravaganza as one newspaper called it.

The Hospice-thon Team - Bill, Trudy, Malcolm and Clive

'Luke FM Radio Station' at the Hospice

Luke FM Radio manager Clive raises his glass to Bill on a Hospice-thon job well done

Bill encouraged, cajoled, 'coerced' hospice supporters, local companies, clubs and individuals to fundraise for St. Luke's.

Bill and his Hospice-thon team were on hand with help and information packs to get them to reach their targets.

We had a special Hospice-thon telephone number, staffed by a team of volunteer operators to take telelphone pledges from the public.

'Luke FM' - our very own Hospice-thon radio station was set up in the kitchen area upstairs of the old farmhouse - the nucleus of St. Luke's Hospice.

The station was managed by Clive Thomas. Clive was a presenter on hospital radio and Radio Caroline - a very gifted broadcaster.

It broadcast live throughout our area giving details of fundraising stories, interviewing our supporters and keeping everyone informed with updates as the donations came in.

The **Hospice-thon** ran throughout the year ending with a gala evening.

Solving The Debt Problem

These Gala Evenings were held amidst great excitement.

Donations were handed in to St. Luke's on stage. We had a large number board which kept altering as the total amount raised grew larger and larger and the cheers grew louder and louder. It was wonderful.

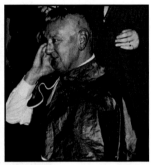

Three brave men faced the scissors for St. Luke's - one lost his pony tail, one had the 'full monty' and even the young came forward to lose their lovely locks for the Hospice-thon

Fundraising Ideas

Auctions	Keep fit events
Antiques road show	Netball competition
Art exhibitions	No smoking day
Aerobatics	Old time music hall
Beard shave	Obstacle race
Bedroom tidying	Penny collection
Bake in	Pulls
Balloon race	Ambulance
Beetle drive	Taxi
Barbecue	Bus
Coffee morning	Lorry
Computer game contest	Pushes
Cover a distance with coins	Bed
Corny joke marathon	Cot
Concert	Pram
Car wash	Pub competitions
Cheese and wine party	Quiz evening
Custard pie throwing	Sales
Darts tournament	Bring & buy

Special Hospice-thon Song

We all sing this to the guests to show gratitude for their support

(To the tune of 'Bless 'em all)

They say there's a Hospice-thon starting right now
In aid of our St. Luke's
So many people all holding events
Raising much money till energy's spent...We
need ev'ry pound that they raise
As we labour both nights and days
To care for our friends, as time with us they spend
Supported by Good Folk like you

Bless you all, bless you all
Eastgate and Tescos and Dales
Sava Centre and the Body Shop too
Councils and slimmers and our friends at Booooots
The darts teams and bowls clubs and pubs
And so many more different clubs
With you on our side, ... we are bound to survive.............
So thank you good friends bless you all

159

Solving The Debt Problem

We solve the 'Debt Problem'

The Debt Busters - Trudy and Bill

Bill organised three Hospice-thon's over the succeeding years and each one was a stunning success.

The first Hospice-thon raised the magnificent sum of **£76,000**

This figure came out very close to our debt figure of **£97,000**. Isn't that amazing?

It meant we were well on our way to solving our debt problem

I like to think it was another **'miracle'** in the miraculous story of St. Luke's.

Thank you God for giving Bill the vision of the Hospice-thon and for everyone who had helped to raise this staggering amount.

'My Boy Bill' had been sent by God to help us solve our problem, of that I am sure.

Of course, Bill would take none of the praise for the outstanding success of his mammoth fundraising projects.

But I know we could not have done it without Bill and his team of volunteers.

The photos on the previous pages are there to give you just a flavour of some of the Hospice-thon fundraising ideas that our community came up with.

Everyone joined in the fun of it.

We had our very own **'Luke'** mascot as a cuddly toy.

I wonder if there are many homes in Basildon, Wickford, Billericay and Thurrock like mine who still have a cuddly toy named **'Luke'**?

Hospice-thon mascot Luke

The Day Care Extension

Need for Day Care Extension

Following more requests for patients to attend our Day Care facility, it soon became apparent that the large lounge area in the hospice was inadequate to care for both In-Patient and Day Care patients.

We were also able to offer more comprehensive care to both In and Day care patients, as complementary therapy and physiotherapy and other areas of care were developing. It meant we needed more space.

As a temporary measure - for a maximum of 1 1/2 years - we moved Day Care into our dining/meeting room.

This obviously meant that staff and volunteers had to find a little space anywhere, mainly in offices, to have their meals.

You would find someone tucked away in the strangest places to enjoy their meal. This really could only be a temporary solution as the nurses still needed to use the In-Patient facilities,

Meals In Unusual Places

bath and treatment rooms to care for the patients' needs and both In-Patient and Day Care staff had to work out a rota with each other so that they didn't clash.

The chapel, situated off the dining room could not be used during this period. So again we had to find any quiet little place for devotion and prayer.

Likewise our study days and external educational talks had to be limited to evenings and weekends.

Les and I, together with the Trustees, met and prayerfully discussed the option of an extension to the Hospice from the dining room area to facilitate day care accommodation.

Day Care Exension Appeal

It was decided to have an appeal for the Extension of the Hospice to build an extra area just for Day Care patients.

We contacted our dear friend and architect Peter Strong about these possibilities.

There was of course, as always, the question of finance. An appeal went out to everyone we could think of.

To members of our community, churches, clubs such as Rotary, Lions, Inner Wheel, to businesses, Schools, - more or less the same process as we developed in the early days.

Our wishes and needs were put to everyone we could think of in the hope they would once again help us.

The Day Care Extension

Prayer Chain Set In Motion

The prayer chain worked overtime, and our faith in God and our Community never failed us, but, of course, we all had to do our bit.

Old contacts were refreshed and generous donations received.

We were, as always, grateful for any contribution, no matter how big or how small. Remember our first donation - Minnie's 25p?

We had several meetings with Council representatives in order to obtain planning permission for the project.

There then followed discussions with officials from the Health Authority, Fire Service and Health and Safety Executive

During this time we still, obviously, had to continue with the financial needs of St. Luke's.

In 1993 the plans were completed and once more we were involved in building work at the hospice.

Extract from my Matron's Report Aug/Sept Oct 94

The Day Care Apppeal is going well and donations are slowly coming in. The leaflets are in the process of being printed.

No doubt the good news has filtered through re the wonderful donation of £35,000 from Mrs Kay Glendinning of the Dunhill Trust to our Day Care Appeal, which I received just prior to going on annual leave to Nepal visiting my brother, thus giving my morale a wonderful boost.

A meeting was arranged with the architect Mr. Peter Strong. Also attending was myself, as Matron, Les, (administrator) and Viv, (Day Care Sister). Mr. Derek Adams was invited to attend to discuss the increased parking

Mrs Kay Glendinning with Gerry Peaty, Hospice Management Committee

facilities which will be included in the building work. Our present car park gets very congested, especially on Day Care days and when holding various functions

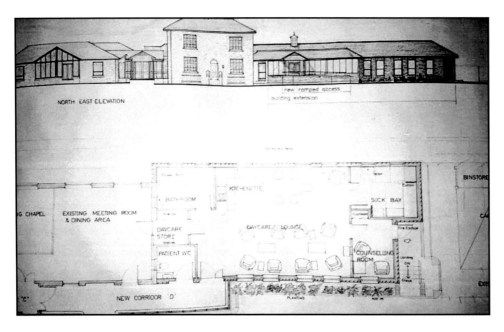

Plans are passed for our new Day Care Extention

The Day Care Extension

Cash drive boosts fund for hospice

ST LUKE'S Hospice's Trudy Cox is driving away with £25,000 — but that's just the half of it!

The cash bonus is the first instalment of a bumper £50,000 raised for the hospice by Wickford Rotary Club.

Club president Harry Payne, and his predecessor Sid Sutton chose to support the charity this year and throughout 1996. And members are confident they will be handing over another £25,000 cheque to the hospice next year.

The money has been raised through a range of events including a monthly quiz at The Chichester, in Rawreth, and a barn dance at Barley-lands, in June, which brought in £1,600.

Founder of the children's hospice at Nether Mayne, Basildon, Trudy Cox thanked the Rotary Club for its efforts.

She said: "This is wonderful. I am very, very grateful."

The money will be put towards the £240,000 cost of building an extension to the day care centre allowing 10, rather than the present six, patients to be looked after each day.

■ Rotarian Harry Payne and the hospice's Trudy Cox get to grips with the cash raised through a Rotary Club fundraising drive

Rotarians Mick Kemp and Harold Payne hand over the first cheque to help us build our new Day Care Extension

The Day Care Extension

Derek and I make sure the hole is deep enough to take a tree

Extract from my Matrons Report Jan/Feb 95

Car Park

I recently met with Peter Strong (Architect) and advised him that Mr. Derek Adams will be overseeing the parking and hardcore area of our proposed car park extension, as well as the removal of the chalets. With Derek's help this will save us a lot of money.

Further Extract from my Matrons Report Jan/Feb 95

After numerous meetings with: The Principal of Basildon College - Mrs Susan Woodrow, the Sports and Leisure Centre Managers, the Council Planning Department, Landscape Department and Principal of Basildon Council - we were granted permission to uproot and replant eight trees, which was done with great enthusiasm, and was quite fascinating to watch. This was carried out under the direction of Derek Adams.

A party of people have been working on the car parking site - including myself (great fun and very therapeutic). Derek Adams is busy contacting various companies re hardcore, sand, mechanical equipment etc and I really cannot praise Derek highly enough for his dedicated efforts to save the hospice money wherever possible. I would greatly appreciate a letter of thanks from the Management Committee to Derek to acknowledge his commitment, enthusiasm and the hard work he has put into this project.

First stage in the building of St. Luke's Day Care Extension, as with any building project, is to clear the site.

This meant eight large 20 foot high mature trees had to be moved and planted elsewhere. "But how were we going to move eight large trees?"

We soon found out. The arrival of the tree moving truck caused quite a stir. But in fact the truck made it look so easy.

First, its enormous bucket on the front end dug a big hole. Then with the same bucket it just dug up a tree and plopped it into the hole.

In no time at all seven holes had been dug and seven trees had been re-planted. On to the next job - moving two wooden sheds to clear the site.

The Day Care Extension

Moving a large shed is no easy matter unless you've got a squad of dedicated shed movers and pushers and a few metal poles to roll it on !

Our hospice garden team soon got to grips with it, helped by a group of volunteers from Ford New Holland.

Further Extract from my Matron's Report Jan/Feb 95

I am sure you will appreciate the time and research that Derek has had to put into locating main underground drains and the careful management of the grounds.

Following my meeting with Susan Woodrow - Principal of Basildon College and her Estates Manager, Eileen, I am still awaiting written confirmation regarding access to the Hospice via the Sports Centre/College car park during building work.

I will chase up sometime next week the possibility of renting/purchasing of the small area of waste land at the Sports Centre/College for storing of our refuse bins and refuse collections.

Following further discussion with Peter Strong, a meeting has been arranged between myself, Peter and the Mechanical & Structural Engineers to finalise actual working plans and requirements.

Peter is now formulating the specifications and this will take approximately two weeks to complete, after which the Tender should then go out, and will take around 4 weeks. We look forward to receiving same, and the day we can finally commence work.

The 'shed moving team' line up for a photo

The Day Care Extension

They say every picture tells a story.... well... this is how we extended the car parking area

First, the rubble had to be broken up - it's just like being in a chain gang

Rubble ready - now for the sand

The sand had to be quite flat, ready to be hammered down

Then came the Tarmac Men

The Day Care Extension

Laying tarmac is easy when you know how

The 'Rubble Gang' toast the new car park

We did it. Well done to all!!

My last photographs here show the 'cutting of the ribbon' to open the car park. and the 'gang' who made it all possible.

We'd re-planted seven trees, moved two sheds and laid an extra car parking area.

What an achievement - and all done by willing volunteers and supporters of St. Luke's, and of course the professional tarmac men, all under the watchful eye of Derek Adams..

I'm always amazed, and very humble, at the way that whenever there is a job to be done, or a problem to be solved, people come forward to help with their skills and their time. And to this day they are still coming forward to support and help St. Luke's.

My thanks to them all. And I will say it again: 'we could not have done it without them.'

The great day had arrived. We could begin the building work of our much needed Day Care Extension.

The Day Care Extension

What a wonderful moment it was when, once again, lorries and diggers arrived at that now famous 'House on the Hill' - St. Luke's Hospice - to commence the building of the Day Care Extension.

Once more we had to put up with all the disruption, mud and mess that comes with new buildings, but it would be worth it.

When the new Day Care was finished it would be so much better for our hospice patients and their families and much easier for our nursing staff.

So we were back in the throes of building at St. Luke's, and loving it.

Although Day Care and the In-Patients staff now had their own part of St. Luke's, they continued to work and share together as colleagues.

The new Day Care extension starts to take shape

The Day Care Extension

Stages in the construction

Our new Day Care Extension is finished.

The Day Care Extension

The moment we were all waiting for:

Breaking through from the old building into the new.

Once this wall was knocked down the Day Care Extention became part of the main hospice building.

Ray was an expert carpenter and made many of the wooden shelving and units you see around the hospice today.

Here he is pictured making sure everything is level for the new Day Care Centre

The Breakthrough - from the new Day Care to the hospice

Ray, our volunteer carpenter

This is how the completed Day Care building looked. It made such a difference, with its spacious interior, to the care we were able to offer to our patients.

The more observant of you will notice we have since refurbished Day Care with a new capet and wallpaper.

Inside Our New Day Care Centre

The Day Care Extension

Canon Roger Royle opens our new Day Care Centre

*Canon Roger declares our new
Day Care Centre open*

*Father Tom, myself, Day Care Sister Viv
and Canon Roger Royle.*

*Official Opening
New Day Care
and Dedication Service*

*Thursday 11th July 1996
4 p.m.*

St. Luke's Hospice, Basildon & District is a Registered Charity No. 289466

1 **One more step along the world I go,**
One more step along the world I go;
From the old things to the new
Keep me travelling along with you:

*And it's from the old I travel to the new;
Keep me travelling along with you.*

2 Round the corner of the world I turn,
More and more about the world I learn;
All the new things that I see
You'll be looking at along with me:

3 As I travel through the bad and good,
Keep me travelling the way I should;
Where I see no way to go
You'll be telling me the way, I know:

4 Give me courage when the world is rough,
Keep me loving though the world is tough;
Leap and sing in all I do,
Keep me travelling along with you:

5 You are older than the world can be,
You are younger than the life in me;
Ever old and ever new,
Keep me travelling along with you.

One of the hymns I chose for the opening service was this one - 'One more step along the way'.

The words, I felt, not only fitted the occasion but also the vision of St. Luke's showing how God has always helped us along the way and is still helping us today.

171

The Day Care Extension

Knees-up Led By Canon Roger

Our Day Care Centre opening was a joyful occasion. With God and our community's help we had again achieved the impossible.

Everyone had every right to be pleased. Against all the odds we had succeeded.

Now our Day Care patients had their own part of the hospice.

It would mean we would be able now to care for an increasing number of people.

It was certainly something to sing and shout about and have a good old fashioned knees up.

And we did - with Canon Roger putting his best foot forward.

Here is a selection of photos of some of the many people who helped us to make our new Day Care facility a reality.

The Day Care Extension

Day Care Sister Viv and myself enjoying a relaxing meal with Heather, Gerry, Kay, Val and Doug

Rev. Michael Woodmansey sharing a Thanksgiving prayer with us.

Peter and Shirley, gifted Christian musicians and singers.

Pat Havens, Matron Daphne Hall and Day Care Dr Barbara Hanson

Ken Sharp, NHS, talking with Pat Stone, 'Evening Echo' Health reporter.

Co-founder, Les, sharing a celebration drink.

173

The Day Care Extension

Pride and Achievement

In the previous pages I've tried to choose a selection of photos to give you a sense of the enormous pride and the tremendous sense of achievement we all felt at having been part of the building of the new Day Care Centre.

We had the keys

We had a bouquet of flowers for Day Care Sister Viv

We had a celebration cake.

St. Luke's Hospice with the new Day Care Extention

The Day Care Extension

Day Care patient Olive leads the way into the new Day Care Centre

With our patients relaxing and enjoying their new surroundings it was time to say goodbye to Canon Roger Royle.

It had been a delight to welcome him to St. Luke's and he brought with him just the right sense of sincerity and good humour to make our Day Care Centre Opening something special.

Thank you, Roger.

Time to Say Goodbye

Dr Elizabeth Leaves

No sooner, it seemed, had we managed to secure our own doctor and put our medical cover in place than a bombshell was dropped.

The sad news was that Dr. Elizabeth told us she needed to resign. Dr. Elizabeth was with St. Luke's for 20 months but the time had just flown by.

Elizabeth had not been very well for a while and we were getting quite concerned.

The daily travelling had taken its toll on her. She had hoped she would be able to sell her house in Eltham and move closer to the hospice but this had proved to be difficult. The one happy piece of news was that she was expecting another baby.

We were very excited for her. Her daughters, Victoria and Rosemarie, were looking forward to having a new brother or sister. It proved to be a new sister, Isabelle.

Because of all the above concerns Elizabeth felt she had to leave St. Luke's. We were devastated. It would be so difficult to find someone who fitted in so well with us all.

Someone who also had her gift in teaching, sharing her skills and knowledge with us.

What would we do without Elizabeth?

We were facing a new and difficult challenge. Elizabeth would be a hard 'act' to follow.

Happy times with Dr. Elizabeth and Rosemarie. In the earlier photo my grand-daughter Danielle helps Dr. Elizabeth give a slide to Rosemarie. In the other photo my other grand-daughter Nicola (right) shares a cake with Rosemarie

Where would we find a suitable doctor and how would we manage for medical cover during the interim?

I prayed hard, "God, please help us".

In true hospice fashion we held a little farewell celebration for Elizabeth and her family.

We couldn't let her leave without us showing our appreciation of her.

We wanted to thank her for all her help, support and commitment to St. Luke's. Not only to me personally but also to my nursing staff.

She was always there for all the hospice 'Family' - administrative staff, volunteers and helpers. Elizabeth promised to continue to think of us and pray for us.

Ruth, one of our Hospice Trustees, handing over our gifts to Dr. Elizabeth.

Dr. Elizabeth, her husband Paul, and her two little girls, Rosemarie and Victoria.

Medical Cover after Dr. Elizabeth Leaves

I was sad that Dr. Elizabeth was leaving us. We had enjoyed a good working relationship and were very privileged to have had Dr. Elizabeth with us from the start of St. Luke's being fully operational.

A very high standard of medical care had been achieved and my prayers were to maintain that high standard.

With Dr. Elizabeth leaving the full responsibility of clinical care once again fell back on my shoulders as Matron of St. Luke's.

I felt very concerned and anxious about the future and I admit, to my shame, that I was very depressed and burdened at that time.

Dr. Elizabeth's last 'On Call' duty was to be on New Years Day. I again quote from my Report:- "I sincerely hope that we receive a good response to this post and are successful in appointing a suitable candidate as soon as possible". Dr. Elizabeth would indeed be a hard act to follow.

In my Matron's report for September/October 1992

I noted that an advertisement for the post of Medical Director had been placed in the British Medical Journal, as well as to St. Christopher's Hospice for display on their various notice boards. Other options we looked into at that time was advertising in a free Hospices' newsletter, such as 'Palliative Care Today'.

Further in my Matron's Report from January 1993

I wrote how fortunate I was to receive much encouragement and support especially from local GPs Dr. Chris Williams, and equally from Dr. Anthony Millwood who was such a help, and always available when needed.

I also received a great deal of reassurance from Dr Colin Trask, Consultant Oncologist at Southend Hospital who offered help and advice should the need arise and we should find ourselves in the situation of interrupted local medical cover.

And, of course, Dr. Graham Tosh, Medical Director of Fair Haven Hospice, Southend, who took on much of the clinical responsibility together with another local GP, Dr. Ron Sharpe and retired chest physician Dr. Barbara Hanson.

We were also very fortunate to have our unsocial hours, weekends, evenings, night time and Bank Holidays covered by consultants, Dr. Lee, Dr. Woodgate and Dr Willoughy from Basildon Hospital.

Each week I made up a clinical rota with the help of all those dear doctors. They were truly wonderful and made me personally very reassured and relieved.

Nevertheless, we still had the thorny problem to grasp of who would follow Dr. Elizabeth as our new Medical Director.

They were very worrying times and, looking back, I believe we only survived with God's help and the backing and help of a very loyal staff and volunteers.

I cannot begin to thank everyone enough for all their help at this critical time, especially our volunteer doctors. Thank you everyone, very very much.

For the next three years we managed on salaried local doctors until we finally managed to replace Dr. Elizabeth.

Dr. Chris Williams

Dr. Colin Trask

Dr. Graham Tosh

Dr. Anthony Millwood

Dr. Barbara Hanson

Dr. Ron Sharpe

My last time with Ken

Ken and I had been friends for a long time. He was a member of the Wickford Fundraising Group. A kind man, one of England's 'Gentlemen.'

He was diagnosed with cancer but finally succumbed to the disease and was admitted to St. Luke's.

As Matron I always tried to greet all patients and staff every morning and then again wished patients and their families who may be still there good night before retiring for the day. This was something I always looked forward too.

Often, when patients arrive at the hospice, distressed, scared, weary and exhausted, and usually in a lot of pain, to see them settled, comfortable and relaxed, made the evening round especially precious to me, knowing we have been able to be a little part of the patient's life when they needed help and support, understanding and patience the most.

I went to see Ken in his bedroom, his name on the door, just his name, indicating that was his home for as long as he needed it.

Although he was sleepy, he welcomed me with such warmth and love, which was very humbling. He always managed a smile, and then we talked, listened and talked.

He thanked me for the vision of St. Luke's and he also thanked me for letting him help to make it possible. He told me how that made him so proud and grateful, but then he asked about me. 'How are you, Trudy, you look tired?' 'Are you ok, not overdoing it?', in his fatherly way.

It was a time when the responsibilities of it all weighed heavily on me. Are we managing to really, I mean, really help these dear patients. Some were dying, some needed pain and symptom control, some were angry and difficult and it was so important to help them.

Some were here just to give their carers a break, Patients filled with guilt of becoming a burden to them. Some were here on their last journey, like Ken. I cared for him so much, there was a special bond and understanding between us.

He was sensitive to my needs although he was so ill himself but he looked at me with such concern, I didn't realise that I was that vulnerable. (I usually manage to conceal how I feel).

He encouraged me to 'press on', as he put it. 'It's a wonderful place, so normal and yet so peaceful. Thank you, Trudy, thank you. I would have liked to have lived a little longer, helping my wife Audrey who needs me and also helping with the fundraising.

"I so love it, but my time has come and although sad to leave I wouldn't have wanted to miss this experience of dying without pain and discomfort, in this lovely place, thank you, Trudy, thank you". and that's when I could not hold on any longer.

I cried .... For the loss of this lovely man, thankful for the privilege of having known him, for his friendship and his encouragement, for his love. He allowed me to be myself and it was ok. I didn't have to be 'the matron', the person 'in charge'.

I was me and together we shed tears but amongst the tears we smiled at remembering some of the funny fundraising times, remembering the people we both knew.

We talked about the time I visited him at home, asking him how he would feel coming to the hospice for a little while to help alleviate his pain and discomfort, making him more comfortable, as well as giving Audrey, his wife, a well earned rest.

All these thoughts and memories came back and we had, even in this sadness, a very special time together. I, for one, will never forget the privilege of being with him, his kindness and encouragement. It was a very, very special time and a great encouragement to me to continue giving my best to the work God had chosen me to do.

Thanking God

Thank you God for the vision of St. Luke's.

For the estate agent who didn't throw me out when I asked him for a house for just 25p. Who listened to me patiently while I shared with him my concern for my patients and their families, their loneliness in illness, their pain and distressing symptoms, lack of facilities to care for them in the way they deserved at the end of their lives.

My concern for their families and their guilt and loneliness that I as a nurse often felt because I wanted to help so much but didn't know how. I needed a safe place, a home, a house.

For Mark and Malcolm, the Corporation Town Planners, for recovering from their shock when they first heard all I had was just 25p, who listened to me while I told my story and then organised the meeting with Harry.

Thank you God for Harry, Chief Executive and member of the Basildon Corporation, who listened so patiently to me, while again I shared my concern. How kind he was to me even when I reminded him that in the Town they were building for us, we had a hospital and maternity Unit for new born babies at the beginning of life, but nothing for the end of life.

That seemed to me a very scary and lonely business in a busy hospital ward or alone at home, without skilled and trained people with you.

Thank God, Harry had a great deal of patience with me while I poured out my heart.

For trusting us enough to let us have this beautiful farm house, then known as Fobbing Farm, the 'House on the Hill', now know as St. Luke's Hospice, for a peppercorn rent until we were able to purchase it from the Corporation.

For our friends in the community, Thurrock and Basildon, who joined with us and, even better, stayed with us even when times were hard, doing all the usual and unusual things to raise the necessary funds to buy the lovely old farmhouse and continued fundraising until there was enough money to start the building work of the hospice.

For the Health Authority and their interest free loan to complete the building work. I thank God for all who helped and supported us in the planning of the actual building and the amenities.

I thank God for my colleagues, family and friends who supported me, put up with me when I was tired and weary and trusted in most of my crazy fundraising ideas (not all of them!), and surrounded me with their support, help and love during good and bad times.

I thank God for the nursing, medical and pharmacy staff, for all our dear volunteers, without whose help it just would not have been possible to plan for the care of our patients and their families.

I thank God for all the staff and volunteers who were here at the beginning and those who have joined us since to give this special care and help to our patients, their families and friends.

I thank God for our patients and their families who allow us to care for them. During these last few weeks while trying to write the "Miracle of St. Luke's", God's miracle, I spent many hours remembering and reflecting while looking through the hundreds of photographs and newspaper cuttings and record of the hospice story.

I look at the dear faces of the patients we were allowed to care for, of all the happy and special moments, of the tears and concerns we shared with them. And then I thank God again for choosing us for this privileged task.

I thank God for the strength to continue in hard times and for the trust people showed in us, even for the hard times, it made us stronger, brought us closer together as a community and to God.

St. Luke's is a miracle, a building started with just 25p and yet has been a place of hope and comfort for many, many patients and their families.

I thank God for teaching us to trust, for giving us faith, hope and love for those in need. For the wonderful people we have met and the friends we have made since the conception of St. Luke's.

I thank God for the vision of St. Luke's.

My Retirement

The year was now 1997 and it was time for me to hand over the responsibility of leading the hospice team.

My hospital consultant had been hinting for a while that I needed to take it easy. It was kind of him to worry about me and now I felt I needed to listen to him. After all, he was the doctor who had saved my life many years previously and had monitored me ever since.

I am often asked if it was difficult for me to give up the hospice.

Of course, I knew I would miss my patients, my colleagues and all the volunteers and the rest of the staff within the hospice as well as in the community and all my many, many friends.

The one thing that made it easier was the knowledge that the patients' care would continue at the high standard it had always been whether I was there or not. The nursing staff and I were together for seven years; learning, improving and caring for our patients and their families, as well as for each other.

They are all very committed to the hospice and with their dedication and loyalty have proved themselves over all these years.

I knew there was one part of my hospice life I wouldn't miss - the overall responsibility of running the hospice. Although always supported by the Hospice Chairman and Trustees, the daily decisions fell on me.

As the years passed, more new rules and regulations, Health and Safety issues and the bi-annual Government Inspection team created more paperwork. Obviously we had to uphold the high standard of care we had set ourselves.

I was delighted to welcome Barry as our first and new Chief Executive. We spent two months 'handing over' time together. I will be forever grateful to him for making it easy for me.

Barry, new Chief Executive with me on my retirement day

The clinical part of my duties - my Matron's role - was put in the capable hands of Sue, my night sister. Her new title was Head of Care. Sue was the ideal person to take over from me. She was not only very correct in all that she did, she had a tremendous calming effect on those around her with every task she undertook. This was a valuable asset in leading the nursing team.

Night sister Sue, helping me read my farewell cards

On my last day at St. Luke's I had the biggest surprise ever. Years before I had mentioned to Viv, sister in charge of Day Care, that it would be great to to enjoy a ride in a horse-drawn carriage, just once in my lifetime.

Would you believe it. I was at home getting ready for my farewelll party when a carriage drew up outside my house to take me to the hospice. Viv remembered! Thank you everyone for my special treat.

Here I am arriving in style by carriage, greeted by family and friends.

My Retirement

Waiting inside the hospice was a large gathering of my colleagues, family, patients, friends, supporters and lots and lots of well wishers.

It was wonderful to see everybody there. Gerry, the Chairman of our Trustees, gave his welcoming address followed by a duet from Peter and Shirley, my favourite singers.

By now I was so overcome, the tears rolled freely down my cheeks.

Gerry, however, soon lightened the moment by presenting me with a special gift from among the many presents overflowing on the table nearby. Everybody at

the hospice knew how much I loved gardening so what better gift could I be given than a brand new garden fork.

Lots of hugs followed mixed with laughter and tears in true hospice fashion.

Chairman Gerry presents me my 'special' gift

It was time now to cut the retirement cake with my sons, Michael, Keith and Christopher, giving me a helping hand.

We still had one task to perform - the group retirement photograph. These pictures seem to be taken at all retirement gatherings so why should St. Luke's be an exception?

At the end of a wonderful day, my carriage awaited to take me home, happy but exhausted.

My two grand-daughters Danielle and Nicola, jumped into the carriage followed by my friend, Heather. (In my photograph Nicola is hidden by her sister Dannielle so I've inset Nicola into the picture)

Thank you everyone for making my retirement such a happy and special occasion.

P.S. After a complete rest for two months I returned part time to fundraising and as P.R. Liaison Officer. I did that for another seven years before retiring completely to officially join the hospice as a volunteer.

I was very privileged to receive the honour of being asked to become the Patron of St. Luke's. I now represent the hospice whenever and wherever necessary by giving talks, meeting people and sharing the history and future development .

It is a role I do enjoy. I never tire of telling the story of St. Luke's and promoting the hospice. After all, that's where it all began all those years ago.

MBE Awarded

Imagine my surprise when I opened my post in 1993 and read a letter stating I had been awarded the MBE.

I must confess I thought at first someone was playing a practical joke on me. But the letter from the Prime Minister's office did look genuine. I still didn't believe it even when my sister, who was with me, pointed out the official looking envelope. The letter went on to say the MBE was being awarded to me for services to the Hospice movement, ie., St. Luke's.

The official looking letter with the news of my MBE

I did feel strongly that without the support of all the people of Thurrock and Basildon St. Luke's would not have happened and I should accept the award on their behalf.

The day of the award was truly amazing.

I travelled up to London by Rolls Royce. This was kindly provided to me by one of my patients, Sidney Timmings,

Sidney was very poorly when he arrived at the hospice. He did recover and went home and always maintained he owed his life to the care he received at St. Luke's.

My' Rolls Royce parked into front of Buckingham Palace with my driver, Kenneth

To show his gratitude Sidney lent me his Rolls Royce for 'my' day. His son, Kenneth, was my chauffeur.

Of course meeting the Queen and being inside Buckingham Palace was wonderful. Even though I still didn't think the award should come to me.

I did feel embarrassed writing about my MBE so I asked my good friend Amanda Walsham if she would write something. She sent me the following and I am grateful to her for that.

"I have been honoured with a request to write an insertion in this book by Trudy about her MBE and the founding of St. Luke's Hospice. As a founder member of St. Luke's Hospice Events Group in 1992 I have spent many happy times with dear Trudy both before and after the opening of her Hospice at Fobbing Farm.

"Perhaps my most momentous and happiest time was when I learned that Trudy had been awarded an MBE. Her compassion has no boundaries and her smile with her wonderful accent (yes, Trudy, we all love it) have supported many a frightened and terminally ill patient.

"Trudy, you have been honoured by this country for your work and dedication. So many of us who support your inspiration to build a hospice in the Basildon area are privileged to know you as we all continue with our never ending fund-raising projects". Amanda

My brother, Gerold and I, in front of the MBE chapel in St. Paul's Cathedral which I am now allowed to use

With my MBE in front of the steps leaing into the Palace.

Diagnosis Cancer

All my working life I have been a nurse and now I suddenly found myself being a patient.

I had nursed many, many cancer patients in the past 26 years. First, as a District Nurse, and then organising Support Meetings and Sitting Service for cancer patients and their families.

And now, here I am, a cancer patient myself, experiencing with my own body what previously I could only imagine my patients were going through. Please, God, please let it not be true.

But it was. Mr Ian Linehan, my consultant, was so kind. He looked at me with such compassion, but nothing could have prepared me. I sat there, looking at him disbelievingly, then he handed me the pathology form with the result of my recent colonoscopy. Bowel cancer. Although I saw it, there in black and white, I still could not grasp it. It just couldn't be true. I didn't feel ill, just scared.

I had spent approximately four months in Nepal nursing my brother with bowel cancer and had only just returned from Germany where we held his funeral, and four months later I have the same. It can't be true. But it was. And now here I was, like hundreds of patients before me - a cancer patient surrounded by kind people but feeling very alone.

He explained my situation again to me and allowed me time to be sad and cry, and cry I did.

But then all I wanted was to go home, to be with my family, my children.

They 'phoned the hospice, our St. Luke's Hospice, the place I worked for and in for quarter of a century, and phoned Christopher, my youngest son, who worked there as Head of Corporate Services.

Accompanied by the Cancer Nurse Specialist, Christopher and I met in between hospital and hospice and there, in the street, we hugged and cried together and then he took me home.

There, my friend Heather was preparing our tea. She previously wanted to come to the hospital with me, but I said, ' Won't be long, half an hour at the most, it's only to get the results of my colonoscopy. See you soon'.

Well, how your life can change from minute to minute. All I could think of was my poor brother Gerold, and my patients who went through it. They must all have felt the same shock and disbelief, and now I am one of them.

But, dear God, I am a nurse not a patient, it's all wrong. But it wasn't.

A dear friend of mine, June, a social worker, who helped us in the early days with training courses and preparing volunteers for the work in the hospice, sent me a lovely letter.

She herself suffered from cancer and later succumbed to the disease but in her lovely kind and humorous way she welcomed me to the Cancer Club telling me 'it is only for exclusive people'.

Mr Linehan, although so very busy, arranged for me to see him a few days later, when I was more composed, to talk to me about the way forward.

He was very kind and explained that he could treat me, but I would end up with a colostomy, but there was a consultant professor at St. Mary's Hospital in Paddington, London, a large teaching hospital, with the latest equipment.

If anyone could avoid a colostomy he feels it would be good to see him. And see him we did, a few weeks later, with me still hoping a colostomy could be avoided.

All my nursing years I had always said, I don't care what happens to me, but one thing I never ever would agree to was to have a 'stoma'.

So quite confidently we went to London to see this famous professor.

He examined me, left me alone for a moment to get dressed and then returned with the news the only way he could help was to give me a colostomy. O, dear Lord, no.

I reacted and behaved badly, crying for myself, my dear brother, who had just died, for all the patients with cancer, for everyone sad and alone.

I think I cried for England, and the world and just couldn't stop.

Diagnosis Cancer

He left Derek and me alone for a moment, then I managed to thank the dear professor for seeing me and agreed to come in for surgery.

Derek and I were planning to get married. He had nursed his late wife with cancer and I didn't want him to go through it again. I was already hurting, so now was the time to end this relationship. One more hurt wouldn't matter now.

Gladly, he didn't want to hear of it. I am so glad and despite my stoma we married a year later.

We now had to tell my children, my boys, Michael, Keith and Christopher, what was going to happen, that I needed a colostomy after all.

They were so kind and sweet as always and loved me just the same.

And now 8 years on, I wonder why I took it so badly. I am alive with lots of energy and love of life, but much more aware than ever of the fragility of life and more grateful for all the good things in life.

The flowers in my garden, the sunshine and the rain, sunset and the stars at night. Thank you God, for giving me another chance.

It isn't the end. The stoma has become part of me, a bit embarrassing at times but with honesty and a sense of humour and great support from Derek, my family, and all my friends and colleagues at the hospice I am doing fine.

Thank you, God, for sparing me, thank you Mr Linehan and my dear professor at St. Mary's, for Derek, my husband, and my children .

> Cancer is a word, not a sentence
>
> Cancer is so limited.
> It cannot cripple love,
> It cannot shatter hope,
> It cannot corrode faith,
> It cannot eat away peace,
> It cannot destroy confidence,
> It cannot kill friendship,
> It cannot shut out memories,
> It cannot silence courage,
> It cannot invade the soul,
> It cannot reduce eternal life,
> It cannot quench the Spirit,
> It cannot lessen the resurrection power.
>
> *Unknown*

I still have a lot of life left in me. There is so much more I would like to do.

I continue to work on a voluntary basis for St. Luke's, giving talks about the hospice, helping and promoting it, so that the necessary funds can be raised.

This allows us to continue to help all those dear patients and their families at their time of need, and support.

Reflections

Looking back now a feeling of total amazement and disbelief overcomes me.

Did we really start this £2.5 million project with just 25p?

Washing milk bottle tops, separating and cleaning tin foil dishes with left over meals, sorting washing and selling jumble and bric-a-brac to raise money to start the hospice building fund.

Sometimes I feel that I dreamt it all or I am an outsider looking in. But there it is - that lovely House on the Hill that has brought love, help and comfort to many people.

I have been fortunate to have been in a profession which gave me such satisfaction and fulfilment.

Thank you, once again, to everyone who believed in the vision, who joined us and worked so hard to make it possible.

Thank you God for health, strength and staying power even when times were tough.

Thank you for St. Luke's Hospice.

**The complete cost of
publishing and printing of
this memoir is my gift to
St. Luke's Hospice.**